DO YOU NEED A
LITERARY AGENT?

THE **WRITER-IN-THE-KNOW GUIDE**
TO A LITERARY AGENT'S ROLE IN THE
PUBLISHING INDUSTRY

ANGIE HODAPP

DO YOU NEED A LITERARY AGENT?
THE WRITER-IN-THE-KNOW GUIDE TO A LITERARY AGENT'S
ROLE IN THE PUBLISHING INDUSTRY

Copyright © 2019 by Angie Hodapp.
Published by Traderscape Publishing.

Edited by Warren Hammond and Mario Acevedo.
Art and design by Angie Hodapp.

Paperback ISBN: 978-1-7335790-0-1
Ebook ISBN: 978-1-7335790-1-8

CONTENTS

INTRODUCTION

WHO IS THIS BOOK FOR?

THE TOP-LEVEL ANSWER IS THAT THIS BOOK IS FOR writers of novels, creative nonfiction, or memoir who are trying to decide if the path to traditional publication is right for them. My aim here is to provide such writers with a bird's-eye view of the traditional publishing industry so that they can make informed decisions about their careers.

More specifically, if you're looking for an in-depth explanation of what literary agents do—and *don't* do—for their author-clients because you want to decide for yourself if you really need one, then this book is for you.

You, as a writer today, have the luxury of choosing among a variety of publishing options...

You can choose to self-publish your work, which means

you or professionals you hire will take responsibility for revision, editing, cover art, and design; file preparation and output for print, digital, and even audio editions; decisions about which platforms to publish through and the launch of your book on those platforms; the marketing and promotion of your book leading up to and after publication; and even the warehousing and distribution of your physical editions.

You can choose to submit your book to small or independent publishers that don't require their authors to be represented by a literary agent. (Note that you'll hear some people in the writing and publishing community use "independent" or "indie" publishing synonymously with self-publishing, while some small publishing companies refer to themselves as independent publishers. Confusing!) These publishers run the gamut when it comes to how many of the above-mentioned tasks they have the budget and resources to perform, and to what extent. They might even ask you, the author, to take on some of those tasks in cooperation with their staff. For some authors, this is ideal because it gives them a voice in decisions about their book's production. Contracts tend to be basic, with little room for negotiation—which isn't to say you shouldn't read and consider them carefully and at least ask for any changes you'd like to see made. Advances tend to be on the small side, if an advance is offered at all, but to compensate, royalty rates might be higher. Royalties could be offered on a traditional model—either a percentage of your book's selling price or a percentage of net ("net" meaning the publisher's proceeds on the sale of your book less expenses they incurred related to those sales). Or royalties they might be offered on a profit-sharing model.

Finally, you can choose to pursue a traditional-publishing deal with a larger, well-established publishing house. In this book, we'll look most closely at traditional deals done with the Big Five—Penguin Random House, Hachette, Macmillan, HarperCollins, and Simon & Schuster—and their many imprints. (Fun fact: The Big Five used to be the Big Six until Penguin and Random House announced their merger in 2012.) Along the traditional path, you'll sell some but not all rights to your book, depending on how your contract is negotiated, to a publishing house, who will then handle all the above-mentioned tasks. Your level of involvement after you sign your contract will vary, again depending on how your contract is negotiated. But because larger publishing houses are fully staffed with professional editors, artists, designers, marketers, and salespeople, and because larger houses have the greatest distribution reach and the most well-traveled inroads to lucrative subrights deals, many writers continue to dream of landing a Big Five deal.

No matter which path you choose now, know that it doesn't have to be your path forever. Plenty of writers started their careers with Big Five publishers, but then moved into self-publishing when it became a viable, lucrative option. Plenty continue to write for both realms, becoming what's known as "hybrid authors." Some writers start out with small-press deals, and then move into Big Five with later books or series. And some writers who started out in self-publishing tire of wearing so many hats and seek out partnerships with small or mid-sized presses or Big Five imprints.

Whatever your goals are, having a team of trusted professionals invested in the success of your book frees you up to do what you do best: write more books!

However, pursuing the traditional path, especially the one that leads to the Big Five, often requires that you secure the representation of a literary agent. And securing the representation of a literary agent is a process that requires persistence and patience.

Traditional publishing is not for everybody. And that's OK.

However, what makes me cringe is when I meet writers who decided to go indie before they fully understood the very different skills, responsibilities, and workloads associated with self-publishing. Often, the decision is made due to impatience with the lengthy pursuit of a traditional-publishing deal, or perhaps they listened to bad advice or alarmist anecdotes passed around among their writing tribes that left them with an incomplete grasp of what traditional publishing is or how it works.

This book exists to help you make informed decisions that are right for you.

That said, this book will not offer much to those looking for information about self- or indie-publishing. There are already tons of fantastic resources out there on that topic. Nor will it offer specific guidance for writers of scripts, poetry, personal essays, magazine articles, short stories, or nonfiction books, the latter of which often require that the author compose a monstrous beast called a book proposal. Plenty of great resources on writing book proposals already exist, too. Again, those who will find this book most useful are writers of novels, creative nonfiction, or memoir. Why? Quite simply, because that's what the agency I work for primarily represents, so those are the channels about which I can provide the most reliable information.

Whether or not you've completed a manuscript, it's never too early to familiarize yourself with the nuts and bolts of the publishing industry. So let's get started.

PART I

LITERARY AGENTS

I

DO YOU NEED A LITERARY AGENT?

IF YOU'RE A WRITER WHO HAS BUILT, OR IS PLANNING TO build, a career as an independently published author and you're satisfied with the workload and the distribution channels that are available to you, then you don't need an agent. Likewise, if you are already publishing with a small or mid-sized press that doesn't require its authors to have agent representation and you're satisfied with that experience, then you don't need an agent.

We do get a handful of query letters each week from authors who have independently published, but either they didn't have a good experience—low sales, limited distribution opportunities, dwindling resources—or they didn't realize how much time, effort, and money they were going to have to devote to running their own publishing company. Now they want some professionals on their team. They've discovered that being an indie author is expensive and time consuming; some have discovered they're in over their heads. As with any business venture, the initial investment is a risk, and when it comes to paying freelance professionals for the developmental editing, copyediting, typesetting, cover art and design, etc., that you will need to make your book a serious competitor in the marketplace, you will get what you pay for. There are no guarantees that even a high-level of initial investment will result in high-level revenues; however, it's a pretty sure bet that a low investment in either time or money will yield low returns.

So now these authors are changing tactics. They're sending query letters out to literary agents, hoping to secure the representation necessary to land a traditional deal.

Can you get an agent to represent your previously self-published work? Maybe. But probably not. I will say that for the agency where I work, we do read and consider queries from previously independently published authors. However, your best bet is to query with something you haven't published yet and that isn't part of a series that includes books you've already published. The best way to catch our eye is to query something totally new and complete and ready to sell.

Despite the long odds, if you do decide to query with a novel that you already published—maybe it's still available, or maybe you pulled it down before you started querying it—then (a) be honest about that in your query letter, and (b) be prepared to wow us with your sales numbers. Not your sales ranking on Amazon—*your numbers*. Life-to-date copies sold is what we're interested in.

I read a query once from an indie author who admitted that her book had only sold five or six copies in its first year, but would we consider representing it to help her reach a wider audience? Would we help her land some foreign-rights deals and maybe a movie option, too?

Put yourself in our shoes. If you were an agent, would you think that taking this author on would be the best investment of your time? Probably not. Maybe the book is amazing, but authors who lead with their failures aren't really representing themselves or their potential as professional writers as well as they should. In most cases, the best move is to write something new and wonderful and submit that instead. Maybe after you impress us, we'll take a look at your previous work.

On the other hand, an indie author who's killing it on Amazon US, who's published a few books, each with weekly unit sales in the thousands, who's established a consistent, recognizable brand and sizable following, who's now looking for subrights representation…that's an author whose query letter we're going to read more carefully. Be aware that at the time of this writing our agents don't take on clients to represent subrights only, but any of them would consider such a client if the right project came along.

2

WHAT DO LITERARY AGENTS DO?

My canned answer to this question used to be, "Literary agents are the Jerry Maguires of the book world, but they represent authors instead of athletes."

Years ago, that would elicit at least some basic level of understanding. Nowadays, however, the Jerry Maguire reference has become obscure, eliciting little more than an understanding of my age. (*Show me the money? You had me at hello?* Anyone? Anyone?) Alas, the movie was released in 1996, which makes it older than some of the writers who are asking what agents do in the first place!

In any case, if my Jerry Maguire reference didn't do it for you, here's a rundown of what literary agents do.

LITERARY AGENTS ACT AS SCREENERS FOR PUBLISHING HOUSES.

Why do publishers need screeners? Well, there's a massive amount of fiction being written right now by an epic number of people who aspire to be published. Everybody has a story. Go to your next big family gathering or class reunion, mention that you're a writer, and count how many people tell you they have an idea for a book. (Politely walk away from those who suggest that you write it for them and then split the profits fifty-fifty, and try not to roll your eyes.)

Far fewer is the number of those who have actually written an entire manuscript.

The job of Professional Fiction Writer is highly sought after, and the Big Five publishers are not structured to handle the veritable deluge of slush (unsolicited submissions) they would receive if they did not work with trusted agents who act as screeners. Therefore, most, if not all, of the Big Five and their many imprints will not consider—will not even *look at*—a manuscript submitted by an un-agented author.

LITERARY AGENTS ARE MATCHMAKERS.

The best agents are relentless networkers who foster professional relationships with editors who are acquiring manuscripts in the genres the agents represent. Agents are always asking editors: *What are you looking for? What are you not looking for? What have you seen too much of lately? Or not enough? Are you sensing any exciting trends emerging? What have you read recently that you wish you had acquired?*

All of this is to say: *What kind of manuscript can I find for you?*

Editors' answers affect how agents read their slush piles—or how they direct their slush readers or query-letter screeners to read their slush piles. For an agent, the only thing better than reading a well-crafted submission is knowing immediately which editor would be its perfect match.

Actually, better than that is the day the author signs the contract!

It's important to note, though, that good agents are matchmaking for the mutual benefit of both the editor and the author. It's best for everyone—and for the life of the book itself, as well as the author's future books—if the author-editor match is a good one.

LITERARY AGENTS HAVE TOUGH CONVERSATIONS SO YOU DON'T HAVE TO.

Sometimes that author-editor match *isn't* a good one. Sometimes the relationship is cordial at best. Sometimes the author and editor realize they're not a good match only after the contracts get signed and the revision process gets real. And sometimes the author-editor relationship works great for the life of an entire series or two, but then maybe the author wants to change it up. Say they were writing young-adult fantasy series, but now they want to write historical mysteries for the adult market. What if that's a genre or market their current editor simply doesn't do? Or what if their editor changes houses or leaves the industry altogether? These kinds of things happen all the time.

This is where a good agent comes in super handy.

Agents stand in the gap. When conflicts or unexpected career obstacles arise, an agent steps up to protect the author's interests.

Let me say that again: *the author's interests.*

That means: *not the editor's or publisher's interests.*

Wait. Didn't I just state that good agents are matchmaking for the mutual benefit of both the editor and the author? Yes, I did! Any deal has to be mutually beneficial; otherwise, why would either party agree to it?

The difference here is that when a tree falls across an author's career path (and if you're thinking about applying for the job of Professional Fiction Writer, then expect a lot of trees to fall across your career path, often with no warning), a good agent will not only be the first one on scene, but they'll be the one who shows up with the chainsaw.

Expect your agent to have tough, uncomfortable conversations with other members of your publishing team on your behalf. This could mean, for instance, acting as an intermediary during discussions about a manuscript's editorial acceptability.

"Editorial acceptability" is a phrase that's standard in publishing contracts, and its meaning, like a lot of things in the publishing industry, is highly subjective. The worst-case scenario is that the editor or publisher evokes the clause to declare a signed contract null and void if at any point before publication they deem the manuscript you delivered to be, well, editorially unacceptable. Not good enough to publish. Conversations about this can get tense.

Other tense conversations happen when your publisher kills your five-book series after publishing only the first two books.

Or they push back your publication date, even though the timeline was agreed upon in your contract.

Or they renege on their promise to make your book a lead title during a particular release season because some other author's shinier debut novel came along.

Or they decide your hardcover edition didn't sell

well so they're not going to release your novel in trade paperback—which is the format in which most books make the most money.

Or they decide not to exercise any of the subsidiary rights that you granted them in the contract (audio, translation, etc.), and now those revenue channels are forever closed off to you.

Or they refuse to revert your rights to you, even after they remaindered all your print editions and hold zero stock in their warehouse.

Yes, expect the trees to fall. And expect that your agent will act in support of *your* decisions in these types of circumstances.

In other words, your agent may have a buddy-buddy relationship with your editor or publisher, but when conflict arises, your agent rises above and acts on *your* behalf, to protect *your* interests.

Whatever the case, the agent not only *makes* the match, but also *protects* it.

LITERARY AGENTS KEEP THEIR EARS TO THE GROUND.

As mentioned, agents stay current regarding which editors at which houses are acquiring which types of manuscripts. But publishing professionals move around a lot. Editors change houses or imprints, retire, get promoted, go freelance, move to different departments, become agents, or leave the industry altogether. Good agents keep their contacts and networks current.

Keeping their ears to the ground means that good agents also attend national and international trade shows and book fairs. These might include the Frankfurt Book Fair or London Book Fair, where international agents and publishers gather to make deals for the translation rights to your books; the Bologna Book Fair in Italy, where international children's-book professionals, including illustrators, gather to make deals; BEA (BookExpo America) in New York City, which is part of the American Booksellers Association; and the ALA (American Library Association) annual conference or midwinter meeting.

Agents might not attend all international book fairs every year, but the face-time they get with foreign co-agents and publishers means only good things for their authors' careers. This face-time keeps agents informed regarding what publishers in other countries are buying in a given season to satisfy their readers' shifting tastes. For instance, agents might know that a certain genre is on the rise in Brazil, but at no time in the near future will it appeal to readers in Taiwan. Or books of a certain length might do well in Germany, but Japan is looking for shorter books. (Fun fact: Written Japanese requires more printed characters on a page than English, which means a Japanese edition of any book will have a higher page count; therefore, publishers in Japan will most likely be more interested in shorter works, or novels that can easily be split into two or three volumes.)

At BEA, agents talk to booksellers, and at ALA, librarians. These professionals are hugely important to agents because they have the most contact with readers. They can often spot a new trend emerging well ahead of the behemoth that is the publishing industry. So an agent's conversations at these events will also affect how they read their slush piles.

LITERARY AGENTS HELP YOU MAKE INFORMED BUSINESS AND LEGAL DECISIONS.

Again, this frees you up to do what you do best: write more books. Not only do agents track what types of books are selling today (and, more importantly, what might be the hot seller tomorrow), but they also pay very keen attention to shifts in the industry's business standards.

In other words, a good agent isn't easily bamboozled by publishing houses who make lowball offers.

Agents recognize a good offer when they see it, and during subsequent negotiations, they know where to push, how to push, and when to ease up, all to make a good offer better, or even great.

These pressure points certainly include the two things most authors want to know about up front: the advance and the royalty rates. Those are important numbers, for sure, but a negotiation includes so much more than that!

Learn to think of each book you write as more than a single artifact—it's more than a story written down and wrapped in an appealing cover. To an agent and a publishing house, your book is a whole laundry list of rights and conditions, all of which *inform* what the advance and royalty rates will be.

So what does that laundry list of rights and conditions include? First, it includes the territories listed in your contract's grant-of-rights clause. Most commonly, the publisher might offer to buy world rights, world English, or North American English.

World rights better mean a higher advance because it means the publisher is asking to control the publication rights to your book in *all* languages, in *all* formats, across *all* foreign markets. As an author, the thing you should be aware of if you're presented with an offer for world rights is that just because the publisher is buying all your rights, it doesn't mean they will exploit them on your behalf. (Note: Day to day, we typically use "exploit" to mean "take unfair or injurious advantage of," but in publishing-contract legalese, it means "make full use of and derive benefit from." Therefore, you want as many of your rights to be exploited as possible to maximize your book's earnings.)

For example, let's say Fancy Publishing House buys world rights to fifty total books for its fall list—yours and forty-nine others. Obviously, it's in the publisher's best interest to exploit as many rights to those fifty books as they can. But limited resources coupled with smart business practices means they will make data-driven decisions about which subrights deals they'll pursue for each book.

The data they use to make these decisions is both quantitative—data that can be expressed in numbers or graphs, often related to sales and earnings of titles similar to yours in various territories or markets—and qualitative. Qualitative data is information they receive directly from other professionals in the industry. For instance, when a French co-agent or publisher tells your US publisher's subrights team, "Horror isn't selling well here lately, so we're not looking to buy the rights to any horror novels anytime soon," then that subrights team knows better than to waste anyone's time or energy submitting your horror novel (or anyone else's) to that market; but maybe your subrights team knows from conversations they had at the Frankfurt Book Fair last year that horror is currently selling really well in Korea and Brazil, so submitting your deliciously creepy haunted-house novel there is worth a shot. Another example: When a German audio-book publisher tells your US publisher's subrights team, "We're really interested in buying the rights to produce older backlist titles in paranormal romance," then your US publisher's subrights team gets busy putting together a list of those rights they still hold, and suddenly your US publisher is presenting you with a shiny new German-audio subrights deal for that paranormal-romance series of yours that originally came out eight years ago. These kinds of things comprise qualitative data that your subrights team will (or should!) act on.

All of this is to say that, of those fifty books on Fancy Publishing House's fall list, your book might end up being low priority for some markets and high priority for others. So while your friend who also sold world rights to this publisher is getting all sorts of foreign-rights deals, you're not. Or vice versa. And the publisher is often—depending on how your agent negotiated your contract—under no obligation to exploit those rights on your behalf or to revert them to you so that your agent can start negotiating some foreign-rights deals for you.

If your publisher doesn't offer for world rights, they might offer for world English. That might mean a slightly lower advance, because it means the publisher is only offering to buy the rights to publish an English-language edition of your book, but they also want to export it to other English-speaking territories, like the UK (plus the 53 countries in the British Commonwealth) and Australia/ New Zealand (ANZ). Your publisher might also want the rights to sublicense your book to other publishers in these territories, who might want to anglicize it—translate it from standard American English to standard British. This means altering some of your word choices, spelling, and punctuation. When your agent gets you a World English deal, they are retaining translation rights on your behalf because, instead of leaving it up to the publisher to exploit those rights, they are planning to possibly do it themselves by working directly with foreign publishers or co-agents to broker what could result in better deals with non-English-speaking territories.

Finally, publishers might make you an offer for North American English rights, which means they are only offering to buy the rights to publish your book in the English language and sell it in English-speaking North America (US and Canada). This will probably bring your advance down even further, but if you sell North American English, it means you are *retaining more rights* that your agent can sell directly on your behalf. And if your agent is a good one who is well connected within the global publishing market, that will probably mean more money for you in the long run.

Understand that this is all highly simplified, and since this isn't a book about rights specifically, I won't go much further into the nuances of deal or contract negotiations. Suffice it to say, your advance and the royalty rates you will earn will be affected by the following:

- The editions of your book the publisher wants to publish. These include but are not limited to hardcover, trade paperback, mass-market paperback, ebook, enhanced ebook (ebook with the addition of sounds, animations, etc.), audio CD, audio download, bundled ebook-plus-audio, and large print.

- The languages into which the publisher wants to have your book translated.

- The territories into which the publisher wants to sell various editions of your book, in English as well as in other languages.

- The subrights the publisher wants to exploit, either in-house or via a license to a third-party entity. These subrights include but are not limited to audio, large print, condensation, abridgement, serialization, graphic novel, collector's editions, and merchandising (action figures, plush toys, posters, lunch boxes, etc.—any non-book merchandise related to your novel or series that the publisher might want to produce, or license to be produced, sell, and ultimately profit from).

- The performance rights the publisher wants to buy. These include the rights to enter into an option or production deal for a motion picture, television show, stage play, screen play, or even dramatic audio play featuring multiple actors and the addition of music and sound effects. And let's not forget the rights to publish a tie-in edition of your novel—those paperback versions published with the actor who portrays your protagonist pictured on the cover.

What's important to note is that each item on the above list is something the publisher *wants to buy from you*. And the more anyone wants to buy from you, the more you should get in return.

Just remember that any initial offer from any publisher, big or small, is going to be a rights grab. Everything I listed above and more will be on the table during a contract negotiation, and this can be overwhelming to authors trying to handle the sale and exploitation of their rights without an agent. Publishers want to buy as many rights to a book as possible for as little money (i.e., the author's advance and royalties) as they can get away with. Writers just want to see their book in print out in the world. In a perfect world, the publisher will exploit all the rights they buy from you, thereby opening up all those revenue channels, which all means more money in your pocket. A good agent knows how to synthesize all these factors and balance the scales to ensure that the final deal points are mutually beneficial for both the publisher and the author.

Besides all this, other conditions that inform the terms of your deal include:

- The genre. The range of standard deal terms for a huge literary tome or sweeping historical saga is different from the range of standard deal terms for a rollicking space opera, cozy mystery, fun contemporary romance, or light beach read. The former types may be expected to win literary prizes, become assigned reading in university literature classes, get picked by celebrity-fronted book clubs, or otherwise appeal to readers for generations to come. The latter types are consumed quickly by their readerships and, therefore, will have a shorter shelf-life; in general, we can predict that their sales will peak and then fall off after, say, one to three years. There are exceptions, of course. Consider the handful of hot urban-fantasy series that took off over the last decade or so, hitting big with readers, then getting made into TV shows, which then drove viewers into bookstores and boosted book sales.

But since no one can predict with 100% accuracy which books or series are going to hit that big, the terms offered in initial publishing deals will most likely fall within the standard range for the genre.

- The market. Just like there are ranges of standard deal terms per genre, there are also ranges of standard deal terms per market. In the fiction world, for example, a picture book will be marketed and packaged differently from a young-adult fantasy. The former must appeal to its readers (young children) as well as the adults in their lives who are making spending decisions on their behalf (parents and other adult relatives, teachers, librarians, etc.). The latter must appeal to teen readers, and although we know plenty of adult readers also spend lots of money buying YA books for themselves, many teens have expendable income and make their own buying decisions; therefore, publishers market YA fiction directly to teens. In general, each category of fiction—from picture books and early-reader chapter books to middle-grade, YA, and adult— will be priced appropriately and can be predicted to perform differently in terms of overall sales and shelf-life. So market will also affect the deal terms an author is offered.

- The initial edition that makes sense for that genre and for those readers. Not all books will be released initially in hardcover, which is expensive to print and expensive to ship, and which comes with a hefty retail price that not all readers are willing to pay. So publishers make careful decisions about which books on their upcoming lists have the best chance of earning back the initial investment they must make to produce and ship hardcovers. Some books will be released initially as trade paperback or mass-market paperback, or even as ebook-only releases.

- Whether the contract is for one book or more than one.

- Whether you're a debut author or a known quantity with a proven track record, and what that track record is.

- Whether or not your agent negotiates a bonus clause for your contract, which is often related to earnings, units sold, or positions attained on particular bestseller lists within a particular period of time (usually one year) after the date of initial publication.

On the subject of bonus clauses: A well-negotiated bonus clause sets a challenging but reasonable goal. In other words, the mark shouldn't be wildly impossible to attain, and your agent will know, based on the genre and market, what is attainable. Bonuses are often, but not always, paid to the author flat out. That means if your book's sales achieve the parameters spelled out in your bonus clause, then your publisher writes you a check for the agreed-upon amount (hundreds or even thousands of dollars), and you receive this money whether your book has earned out its initial advance or not.

Good agents also know how to spot tricky contract clauses that can spell trouble for their authors down the road. This is especially true for agents who have been in the business long enough to have watched publishers' boilerplate contracts change over the years. Publishers don't make small, inconsequential tweaks to their boilerplates. They have *reasons* for swapping "and" for "or" in your out-of-print language. For adding or striking that seemingly harmless little phrase to your competing-works clause. Even the omission or addition of a simple comma can lead to—*and has!*—conflicting interpretations of contractual terms that end up getting hashed out in a court of law.

Good agents not only spot those boilerplate alterations, but they know the right questions to ask when challenging the publisher to explain their reasons for making the change. Good agents anticipate the impact that change may have not only on this deal, for this author, but also for the next deal they do with this house for future clients.

Some agents have backgrounds in the legal profession, but many do not. Regardless, the good ones have an intellectual-property attorney on retainer whom they can consult when they run into a legal snag regarding the handling of your rights.

LITERARY AGENTS GET YOUR MANUSCRIPTS IN SHAPE.

This doesn't mean you can start sending out query letters before your manuscript is, in your best, most honest estimation, 100% ready for publication. Agents will occasionally take on a fixer-upper—a manuscript that isn't quite ready for the market but that promises a unique premise, conveys a strong voice, or delivers a memorable emotional impact. But agents won't make a living if they take on a full slate of manuscripts that need substantial work.

The strongest, most ready-to-publish manuscripts are still the most likely to get picked up for representation.

Still, agents do want to ensure that every manuscript they send out on submission is as strong as possible. After all, once they take you on, they're tying their own professional reputation to your work. If you're thinking like a good agent, then you're thinking, "I want every editor to push aside everything else on their desk every time I send them a manuscript. I want them to know I'm an agent who will not waste their time. I want them to beg to be on all my submission lists!"

There are many agents in the field right now, but few are so consistently on-point that their submissions get automatically shuffled to the tops of editors' slush piles.

That said, some agents are more editorially minded than others. Several of my writer friends are, or have been, represented by agents who have kept them in revision hell for years. I think this happens for one of several possible reasons, none of which are particularly fun for writers to think about:

- Maybe the agent signed you thinking your manuscript was a fixer-upper, but after several editorial passes, you're still not delivering the product they hoped you would. And maybe now, after so many changes and revisions, both you and your agent have lost sight of your original vision for the work. Or maybe your respective visions for the work never really aligned in the first place.
- Maybe the agent doesn't know how to effectively communicate the issues they have with your prose, story logic, character development, or structure. The ability to detect, articulate, and propose viable solutions to these issues is rare,

and just because someone has "Literary Agent" printed on their business cards doesn't mean that editorial direction is one of their strengths.

- Maybe the agent is gun shy. Maybe they're afraid of rejection. Agents experience professional highs and lows just as writers do. Maybe they haven't brokered a major deal in a while and they're starting to worry they aren't cut out for agenting. So they keep you doing editorial busywork, even in the absence of any forward progress—for either of you.

- Maybe the agent signed you as a client and got you going on a revision, but you took too long to deliver the final draft, and any urgency or excitement they felt when they took you on has fizzled. Worse, maybe they know the market has moved on without you.

- Or maybe the agent really does believe that sending you back to the drawing board again and again is actually getting your manuscript closer to submission-ready.

Whatever the reason, if your agent asks you to revise your manuscript more than three times, then it's time for a serious talk. A good agent will initiate the conversation, and they'll be honest about why they're not taking your manuscript out on submission.

A bad agent will avoid this uncomfortable conversation and get you going on more busywork.

A good agent will say, "Hey, this isn't working, and here's why, and I can't sell it because of reasons X, Y, and Z. But send me five ideas and we'll talk about what you should write next."

A bad agent will hedge and evade and keep sending you back to square one.

If you're not a debut author, be aware that there is such a thing as The Curse of the Sophomore Novel. Or maybe it's the sophomore trilogy or sophomore series that's cursed. Ask a handful of traditionally published authors if they've experienced this, and I'm guessing most will tell you they have. I'm also guessing that most who say they haven't are lying.

In any case, The Curse is a common phenomenon that manifests when a writer—for lack of a better way to put it—forgets how to write. Their first book, trilogy, or series comes out to critical acclaim. Success! Then the author delivers their second effort, and the agent sees that everything they thought the writer knew about prose, character, story, and structure has flown the coop.

Why does this happen? One possible reason is that most writers, before they were agented or published, had years to write and revise their first effort, but now that they're under contract, they're rushing through the writing process, or they're laboring under the pressure to write good books on deadline. (Note that most multi-book contracts specify that the author has twelve months to write and deliver an editorially acceptable manuscript, so once you become a professional fiction writer, prepare yourself for that expectation.) Another possible reason is that some writers have only one good story inside them.

Here's the reason I tend to believe is most often to blame: These writers are experiencing a crisis of confidence, whether too little or too much. If too little, they're overthinking and stressing themselves out about their ability to replicate or exceed their debut success. If too much, they no longer think they need to bear the basics of craft in mind.

Either way, a good agent will help an existing client rehabilitate a broken manuscript, even if the same broken manuscript submitted by an unknown author through the slush pile would have been a no-brainer of a rejection.

Agents always give their existing clients more time and energy than they give their slush piles. It follows that an agent suddenly faced with five manuscripts newly delivered by existing clients is going to fall behind on their queries, and they're probably not going to be signing any new clients during the weeks that follow.

So, yes, maybe your query got rejected by Agent X simply because you happened to query her while she was neck-deep in client manuscripts. How would you ever know that? You wouldn't. That's one of those little timing things you can't control. What you can control is getting your manuscript into publishable shape and querying anyway.

LITERARY AGENTS PROVIDE COUNSEL AND GUIDE YOUR CAREER.

Your agent is your cheerleader. When you suffer one of those crises of confidence, your agent will help you come up with a plan to get you back on track. When life gets in the way of a big contractual deadline, your agent will advocate for you in negotiating new deadlines and release dates with your publisher. When you wrap up a series that represents the work of several years of your life, your agent will steer you toward your next project, whether your goal is to land on a bestseller list, switch genres, or write the unconventional book of your heart.

A good agent will also be honest with you and tell you when you're getting in your own way. They'll tell you when you need to calibrate your expectations related to sales, earnings, contract terms, relationships with editors or publishers, and future projects.

Your agent wants you to succeed, because the only way an agent can be successful is to have successful clients. So think of your agent as your number-one advocate and partner in the ever-shifting world of publishing.

LITERARY AGENTS ADHERE TO THE AAR'S CANON OF ETHICS.

Whether or not an agent is a member of the Association of Authors' Representatives, good literary agents conduct themselves in accordance with the AAR's ethical guidelines.

There are a couple reasons why reputable, legitimate agents are not (yet) qualified for AAR membership. One, agenting is not their primary professional activity, or two, they are new to agenting and actively building their client lists, but they haven't yet been the principal party responsible for executing five publishing agreements (contracts) in an eighteen-month period.

If you choose to sign with an agent who is not an AAR member for reasons other than those, then keep in mind that you have no recourse if that agent conducts themselves unethically. And reputable agents do get outed for unethical practices once in a while. In recent months alone, the publishing world has witnessed agents fabricating Big Five offers they then counsel their clients not to accept—most likely to make it appear to their clients as though they are doing their job when perhaps they are not, or as though they are still relevant with Big Five editors when perhaps they are not. Recent allegations have also been leveled against agents for sharing manuscripts with editors when they do not have the right or permission of the authors to do so. Other agents have been outed recently for ghosting their clients—for simply disappearing, no longer answering their calls or emails.

Sad but true, and when agents pull unethical stunts, they cast a pall over the whole profession. Please check out www.aaronline.org to read the AAR's complete canon of ethics, but in the meantime, be aware that compliant agents do the following:

- Respond promptly to clients' emails or phone calls, usually within a day or two.
- Promptly furnish relevant information the client requests, including lists of editors to whom a manuscript has been submitted, copies of responses received from those editors, and documentation related to payments and accounting.
- Pay clients no more than ten days after their receipt of monies.
- Keep clients' personal and financial information confidential.

Likewise, compliant agents *do not* do the following:

- Charge clients or potential clients fees or accept gifts or perks for reading or editing submissions, or for carrying out any other duties of their job.

- Benefit financially other than through the sale of authors' rights. Agents don't charge you money for anything, and they don't get paid until you get paid. They are paid on commission, usually 15% of the gross revenues payable to you, the author, as a result of the deals the agent brokers on your behalf. (Note that commissions vary for subrights deals.)

3

WHAT DO LITERARY AGENTS NOT DO?

At the end of the last chapter, we looked at the number-one thing agents do not do, but it bears repeating: *Agents do not charge authors any money up front for any reason.* Any "agent" who does is not an agent. Turn and run.

Here are some other things agents do not do:

LITERARY AGENTS DO NOT PURCHASE RIGHTS TO YOUR BOOKS.

They simply broker the deals though which you sell your rights to your publishers. This is done with your permission, which you granted them when you signed their agency agreement upon accepting their representation.

LITERARY AGENTS DO NOT PUBLISH, WAREHOUSE, OR SELL YOUR BOOKS.

They are not themselves publishers, and while good agents are more involved than others in working with your publishing house's marketing and publicity teams to ensure that each book you write enjoys a successful and lucrative release, agents are not obligated to assist you with promotion. It certainly benefits them to assist you (more money for you, more money for them), or perhaps help you brainstorm some things you could do to boost sales, but ultimately this is not their job. It's the job of the publisher they helped you sell your rights to. Or it's your job as the author; after all, no one is more qualified to get people excited, whether in person or through social media, to read your book than you are.

LITERARY AGENTS DO NOT EDIT YOUR BOOKS BEFORE SIGNING ON TO REPRESENT YOU.

However, there is such a thing as a revise-and-resubmit, often referred to as an R&R. This happens when an agent reads a submission that's pretty darn good, and although they're not ready to offer rep on it quite yet, they are willing to read a revision. In this case, the agent may provide some fairly specific editorial direction and then explicitly invite the author to submit the revised manuscript for a second read. Here are four things to know about R&Rs:

- If you receive an R&R, you are not obligated to make the changes and resubmit the manuscript. You can simply say thank you and keep querying other agents.

- Be honest about whether you actually received an R&R. An agent who responds to your query with something like "This isn't quite right for me but I'd be willing to read other work from you in the future" is not offering you an R&R. They just rejected you in an encouraging manner and invited you to keep them on your submit list. In this case, don't resubmit *this* work to that agent (unless you spend at least six months completing a thoughtful revision that you honestly believe makes it a far better manuscript), but do submit your next novel if at that time you're still on the hunt for an agent. I've processed plenty of submissions in which the author claims to have received an R&R from one of our agents. However, we keep notes on such things, and often these authors have either misunderstood an encouraging rejection or they've fibbed to gain an advantage in the slush pile. *Don't fib in the slush pile*, whether about an R&R, a referral, an offer of rep from another agent, or anything else. Such tactics don't work, and when you get found out, it makes you look bad. This is a relatively small industry, and agents talk. Keep your professional communications honest and above board from the get-go.

- Agents are wary about putting too much work into an R&R because authors are not required to give them an exclusive read on the revised manuscript. In other words, authors can use Agent A's R&R notes to improve a manuscript, but then take that manuscript to Agent B and sign with them instead.

- An R&R does not guarantee you an offer of representation. You might deliver a revised manuscript that doesn't quite line up with what the agent was envisioning or didn't quite address the concerns outlined in the R&R. Or you might deliver your revised manuscript too late. If it takes you more than a year to deliver an R&R, then maybe the market shifted while you were revising and now you've missed that particular boat. Or maybe the agent now has concerns about how long it takes you to deliver a revision. On the other hand, maybe you delivered your revised manuscript too quickly—a day or two isn't enough time to really nail a thoughtful revision.

In general, if the agent wasn't ready to offer you rep the first time around, then the work they're expecting you to put into an R&R is substantial. If the agent doesn't include a deadline in their R&R, then, depending on how much time you have in your work week to devote to your writing, it's generally OK to take several weeks or months to deliver your revised manuscript. In any case, know that just as you are not obligated to submit your now-stronger manuscript to the agent who gave you the R&R, they are not obligated to offer you rep. Think of an R&R as a very strong maybe.

LITERARY AGENTS DO NOT MAKE PROMISES THEY CAN'T KEEP.

They do not promise to sell your book. They do not promise to net you a particular advance, or, for that matter, to net you *any* particular deal terms. They do not promise you a standard of living that will allow you to quit your day job. They do not promise you that you'll make a bestseller list or hit a particular sales threshold. Good literary agents can speak intelligently about possibilities, but they don't deliver particulars until such particulars are offered by a publisher in writing.

LITERARY AGENTS DO NOT PROVIDE TAX ADVICE.

At least not beyond, perhaps, advising you to hire an accountant to help you navigate the tricky laws and regulations that affect how the IRS views a writer's income and how you will need to file your taxes from year to year.

LITERARY AGENTS DO NOT LEND YOU MONEY.

Self-explanatory. Moving on.

LITERARY AGENTS DO NOT STRIVE TO BE YOUR FRIEND.

The relationships that develops between writers and their agents range from all-business, to polite, to mutually respectful, to friendly, to *my agent was my maid of honor!* Bear in mind that when those trees I mentioned earlier start falling across your career path, you might want someone closer to the all-business end of the spectrum to be the one who shows up with the chainsaw.

That's not to say you can't be friends with your agent. Just don't expect "friend" to be a role your agent plays in your life. Over time, friends, like family members, are less likely to be honest with you about your writing and your career potential. Friends don't want to hurt your feelings. Friends want to be nice to you and make you feel good.

It's good to be simpatico with your agent, but when the chips are down, it's better to have dispassionate professionalism on your side.

PART II

TRADITIONAL PUBLISHING IN 16 EASY STEPS

STEP 1

IDEA

Every novel that made its way from the writer's imagination to the reader's hands got there in its own unique way. Even established writers who have had dozens of novels published will tell you that their journey with each book was different.

Still, it's useful to get a bird's-eye view of the traditional-publishing process and what you can expect from your agent at each step along the way.

Step 1, of course, is that you, the writer, get an idea. Where the idea came from or how well developed it is when it first occurs to you is irrelevant at this point. Let's just say you have an idea, and now you have to turn it into a marketable product.

STEP 2

WRITE THE PITCH

You might have expected step 2 to be write the book. But no! Once you have your idea somewhat fleshed out, now is when you write the back-cover copy (also known as flap copy) or the query pitch. This is the one-to-three paragraph description of your story that is designed to whet the literary appetites of all who read it and make them beg you to take their money.

In all seriousness, a good query pitch is a brief passage of marketing copy. Its sole function is to sell your book—first to agents, then to editors, then to your publisher's sales force, and then to subrights entities, bookstores, librarians, and, ultimately, readers.

No pressure, right?

Most novelists find that writing a good query pitch

is daunting. If that's you, don't worry—you're not alone. We won't dive into the intricacies of crafting a solid query pitch here, but if you want to know more on that subject, please check out my book *Query Craft: The Writer-in-the-Know Guide to Getting Your Manuscript Read,* available in 2019.

For now, just understand that writing your query pitch before you begin working on your manuscript helps you test your idea. Do you actually have a *story*, or is your idea still just a premise, an evocative problem, an interesting world, or a vague image in your mind of a strong central character? If you do have a story in mind, can you pitch it in such a way that it comes across as exciting and fresh? Does your story deliver the tropes that readers of your genre expect while also delivering something unique or interesting that those readers haven't seen before? If so, then taking the time to write the manuscript is a worthy endeavor.

The bottom line is, if your goal is to secure a career getting your novels published by traditional publishers, then you need to practice thinking not only like the artist or creative wordsmith that you are, but also like a businessperson. Get used to the notion that your books (and later in your career when you're selling future novels on synopses, your *ideas* for books) are commodities, and, like it or not, that's how they will be treated in the publishing industry. Your hope is that agents, acquiring editors, and publishers will connect emotionally with your story (there's a reason "you cry, you buy" is a saying in the industry), but at the end of the day, the questions they're asking themselves are: *How many readers will this book appeal to? Can this book compete with what's already available to readers? Is taking on this book a smart business decision?*

Writing your back-cover copy or query pitch before you write your manuscript helps you not only test the marketability of your idea, but also see where your idea might need to be fleshed out or fine-tuned. It helps you see if your story idea is complete before you begin writing it.

Once you've written your pitch, must your manuscript stick to it? Absolutely not. Fiction has a magical way of taking on a life of its own, and for a lot of writers, the best ideas come during the writing itself, not during the story-planning stage. So honor that magic!

However, fiction also has a tricksterish way of pulling its author into the weeds, where plot and story logic wander off and get lost. If that's a problem that sounds familiar to you, then having a solid pitch to return to can help you nudge the story back onto the original track you laid.

STEP 3

WRITE THE BOOK

It doesn't matter if you're a pantser (someone who writes by the seat of their pants) or a plotter (someone who outlines the whole story before they begin to write it). It doesn't matter if you're a one-draft-and-done writer or an I'm-on-my-eighteenth-draft-and-I-think-I'm-starting-to-figure-out-the-story writer. It doesn't matter *how* you get your book done.

What matters is that you get it done.

More to the point, it matters that your novel eventually becomes structured in such a way that readers' brains recognize it as *story*. (For more on how to do that, read *Wired for Story: The Writers Guide to Using Brain Science to Hook Readers from the Very First Sentence* by

Lisa Cron, and check out my other favorite resources in the appendix.)

For this to happen, you need to *understand* story and then be able to *deliver* one, along with all the elements that go into creating and shaping it. *Plot. Structure. Scene craft. Character. Point of view. Dialogue. Description. Goal. Motivation. Internal conflict. External conflict. Tension. Stakes. Voice. Narrative style. Pacing. Turning points. Twists. Cliffhangers…*

I could go on.

The point is, writing a well-crafted book is a major juggling act that requires writers to keep a lot of bowling pins in the air. This can quickly get overwhelming. Enter Step 4.

STEP 4

LET OTHERS IN

LETTING OTHERS IN MEANS YOU MUST FIRST RECOGNIZE that our idealized view of "novelist as lone creative genius" is a highly romanticized myth. If you want to be successful in this industry, then make peace with the fact that *every* writer, no matter how prodigious their past successes, has space to learn and improve. Those who fill that space with other people who can provide honest feedback will probably learn and improve faster than those who don't.

So let others in. Take classes. Sign up for workshops. Read books on plot and structure and character development and all the other aspects of story that you'll need to master. (Again, check out the appendix for a list of my recommended resources.) Enter contests that include a judge's critique in the entry fee. Join a critique group. Find a mentor. Seek out a couple of beta readers—people *you're not related to* who will read your manuscript in full and give you honest feedback.

In short, get lots of people to read your stuff before you send it out to industry professionals. You definitely don't want the first person who sets eyes on your work to be the agent you're hoping will represent you. To agents and their slush readers, stories written behind closed doors by writers who work in isolation are often painfully obvious as such.

Getting people to read your stuff also helps acclimate you to accepting criticism along with praise. It thickens your skin, and that's a good thing.

Get over the idea that asking for help, input, or feedback means you're not a creative genius. On the contrary. Recognize that letting others in might be the closest thing to a shortcut there is in an industry where there are no shortcuts. At least not reliable ones.

By the way, Step 4 can happen either concurrently with Step 3 (write the book) or after Step 3. Some writers find it more useful to get help along the way. They want an immediate course-correction when a bothersome plot hole shows up; when they write their characters into a corner and don't how to write them back out; when they start slogging through the plot's mushy middle and need help pulling the narrative tension tight again; or when a secondary character shows up, demanding the spotlight and hijacking the plot. Having a team of other storysmiths on hand can be extremely helpful for these writers.

Other writers, though, need to work (or battle, tiptoe, sprint, hack, crawl, slog…choose the verb that best describes your process) their way to the end of a manuscript on their own before inviting others into their creative headspace. That works too. Either way, it's the *letting others in* part that counts. So don't skip this step.

STEP 5

QUERY

IF YOU COMPLETED STEP 2, THEN YOU ALREADY HAVE your query pitch or back-cover copy written, right? Ha! Chances are, a thing or two about your story changed along the way. That's OK! Tweak your pitch, or trash it and rewrite it, if you must, to make it reflect the story that your final manuscript ended up telling. Either way, you're ready to write your query letter and start sending it to agents in hopes one might take an interest in representing you and your manuscript. For more information on writing your query letter, please check out my book *Query Craft: The Writer-in-the-Know Guide to Getting Your Manuscript Read,* available in 2019.

STEP 6

REJECTIONS AND REQUESTS

You'll definitely get rejections. All writers get rejected; it comes with the territory. But if your query letter did its job, then you'll get some requests, too.

Some agents will request sample pages—maybe the first ten, maybe the first thirty, maybe the first five chapters. Whatever they ask to see, send it.

Other agents might jump right in and request your full manuscript. That's either simply how they do things, or it's because they were so excited about your query pitch (they found it particularly unique, fresh, or timely) that they decided to skip right over the sample-pages part and get right to your full. Hopefully, it's the latter!

Note that if you're getting lots of requests for sample pages, but your sample pages aren't getting you requests for fulls, then the problem isn't with your query. If only it were. The query is so much easier to fix! No, your query is doing its job—it's your sample pages that aren't doing theirs.

That means the problem lies in some aspect of your execution: your mastery of language and competence with its mechanics; the power of your voice; your ability to immediately hook the reader without frontloading your opening pages with sluggish backstory and awkward exposition; your talent at casting the spell—delivering an evocative story space the reader wants to sink into or a character whose plight the reader can't tear their eyes away from.

Whatever the case, Step 6 tends to require a lot of patience. It's easy to spin-out in your own head, Twitter-stalking the agents you queried and refreshing your email every fifteen seconds. Try not to waste too much time doing such things. The biggest favor you can do for yourself at this point is take some deep breaths and get to work on your next book. Too many writers wait for their first book to sell before they write their second. But what if you do land an agent and the manuscript still doesn't sell to a publisher? Then your agent is going to ask you what else you have ready to shop, so have something else to put in the hopper.

Agent Kristin Nelson says that, on average, her

clients wrote three or four books that didn't sell before they wrote one that did. For some, it was more! If you're in this for the long haul, like Kristin's clients, then buckle in and prepare yourself to write a lot of books. More importantly, make peace with the fact that not everything you write is going to sell.

What's important to take away here is that writers who constantly produce new work are the ones who tend to achieve long-term success.

STEP 7

OFFER OF REPRESENTATION

CONGRATULATIONS! THIS IS HUGE! YOUR OFFER OF REP might start with a phone call—a getting-to-know-you conversation during which the agent might ask you about your writing, your aspirations, your work habits, your long-term goals as a writer, etc.

This is also your opportunity to ask the agent questions that help you decide if *they* are a good professional fit for *you*.

It's easy for newer writers to get so excited by their first offer of rep that they neglect to slow down and think critically about the professional relationship they are about to forge. Questions you might consider asking a prospective agent include:

- What is your communication style?

- If I call or email you, how long should I expect it to take to hear back from you?
- How would you describe your dream client?
- How many clients do you currently have?
- What is your editorial vision for my work?
- How much revision do you think I need to do before the book goes out on submission?
- What would your submission strategy be for this book?
- What happens if my book doesn't sell?
- Are you open to me writing in different genres?
- How long does it take for your agency to negotiate a contract?
- How involved will I be during the deal and contract negotiations?
- Will I have a chance to compare the original contract offered by the publisher to the contract version that you negotiated?
- Will you explain any parts of the contract that I don't understand?
- What can I expect from your agency in terms of accounting support? How carefully do you look at your clients' royalty statements looking for accounting errors? Can you help me read and understand my statements?

- What support staff do you employ and what do they do?
- How would you describe your typical work week?
- Can I chat with one of your clients?

If you don't have a good feeling about the conversation or the agent's answers to your questions, then it's probably best that you don't sign with that agent. I know that's easier said than done, especially if you've been riding the query roller coaster for a long time. It's difficult not to think, *But that's that only agent who wanted me*, or *Getting an agent—any agent—is the only thing I've ever wanted! Just hand me a pen and point me to the dotted line!*

However, most writers who've been in the game awhile will tell you that having no agent is better than a having bad agent.

Again: *Having no agent is better than having a bad agent.*

Don't sign over control of your career or your intellectual property to someone who gives you a bad feeling. Just don't.

Now that that's out of the way, let's look at a sunnier scenario. Let's say you have more than one agent interested in signing you. This definitely puts you in the driver's seat. You'll want to take your time interviewing each agent and choosing the right one for you.

My advice here is that you base this choice on professional considerations. Don't pick the friendliest agent just because they were the friendliest, or the agent whose kids are the same age as yours, or the agent who went to the same college as you, or the agent who has a Dachshund and oh-my-gosh you had a Dachshund when you were growing up.

There's certainly something to be said for positive rapport and feeling a genuine personal connection, but in the end, this is *your career,* and your books are *your intellectual property.* Don't sign the management of your professional future over to someone you don't fully trust, and don't confuse geniality with industry savvy or willingness to go to bat for you and have tough conversations on your behalf. In the long run, the go-to-bat agent is the type of agent you need.

Another thing to keep in mind if you receive more than one offer of representation is editorial direction. You might be tempted to sign with the agent who tells you your manuscript needs the least amount of work. But hit the pause button here. Really listen to each agent describe their vision for your book and the work they suggest you do to improve its chances of breaking out in the marketplace.

Obviously, you don't want to sign with an agent whose vision is drastically different from yours. But don't dismiss the agent who's proposing another hefty revision, especially if you know deep down inside that their suggestions will take your book from *good enough* to *great*.

A good-enough book will get to the shelf faster. A truly great book will live longer. It will earn more readers, more word-of-mouth, more industry buzz, more sales, more favorable reviews—and all of that means more publishing contracts with higher advances and royalty rates for you and your future books.

Regarding agent revisions, here's my caution that bears repeating: Your book needs to be in Grade-A shape before you start querying. I've heard many aspiring authors at conferences say things like, "When my current draft is done, I'm just going to start looking for an agent who will help me revise it. That's what agents do."

Except that's *not* what agents do. Not really. Your agent is not your critique partner. They can't make a living helping you write a Grade-A book. They can, however, make a living helping you turn your Grade-A book into an A-Plus book. Know the difference.

STEP 8

AGENCY AGREEMENT

If you find an agent you want to sign with, this is when you literally sign. The agency agreement is a contract that protects both you and the agent and legally clarifies some important aspects of your future relationship.

Know that there are some very sketchy, unethical agency agreements out there. Read your agency agreement carefully. If you don't understand something in the agreement, ask. Do not sign it until you understand it in full.

In general, here are some things to be aware of when you're considering signing an agency agreement.

First, be sure that it stipulates that either party—you or the agent—can terminate the relationship, and that the termination will be official within a reasonable amount of time (say, thirty days). Some agency agreements might allow you to terminate the relationship but bind you from finding other representation for a crazy amount of time: months or even years. *Years!* Can you imagine? That's a long time for your career to be bound up in a relationship that is no longer working, with an agent who is no longer interested in acting on your behalf.

There is one reasonable exception. Since agents do a lot of leg work on a client's behalf during the early part of that client's career, the agency agreement might ask that you to stick with the agent for at least a year or two. The agent is promising to invest their time and talents in you and your writing, and good-faith reciprocity means you'll stick with them for at least some preliminary period of time. So a good agency agreement might say something like this: *Either party may provide the other with written notice of termination of the relationship, such notice not to be submitted earlier than [period of time] following the date of this agreement, and such termination to take effect thirty days after the date of the written notice.*

The agency agreement will also spell out which rights to which of your intellectual properties the agent is (and isn't) signing on to represent and states that the agent will make best efforts to sell those rights. For instance, if you write both novels and screenplays, you might be signing with an agent who only represents novels, so the agency agreement might, for the avoidance of doubt, state that the agent has neither the right nor the responsibility to help you sell your screenplays.

Make sure that this part of the agreement also states that if the agent chooses not to represent (i.e., attempt to sell) one of your future works, for whatever reason, you are free to shop, sell, or self-publish those works at your discretion.

Here's one scenario where this is important: Let's say you sign with an agent who wants to represent your series of political thrillers, but you also write picture books for children. What if your new agent doesn't represent picture books? What if they have no editorial contacts in that market space? Then your agent might allow you to seek dual representation. You'd have *two* agents, one for each genre or market you're writing in, and you'd want to be sure each agency agreement is very clear about everyone's rights, responsibilities, and claims to commissions on your earnings.

Note that not all agents will be open to spelling out a dual-representation situation in their agency agreement, and do not ask for one unless (a) you are already producing meaningful bodies of work in two different genres or for two different markets, and (b) those genres or markets are so far removed from one another that the line between them has no chance of getting blurred, thus preventing foreseeable conflicts of interest for everyone involved.

Here's another scenario: Your agent sells your first book and everyone is happy. But you write a subsequent book that your agent tells you needs a lot of work. Maybe you have an editorially minded agent who works with you on developing the manuscript, or maybe you don't. Either way, the work isn't shaping up to be something the agent wants to attach their name to, so they break the news to you that they're not going to shop it. At this point, you'll have to decide whether you want to (a) sever ties with this agent and start looking for a new agent, which means you'll be back to querying again, (b) sever ties with this agent and go indie from here on out, (c) stick with your agent, but either self-publish this particular book or shop it to small or mid-sized presses that don't require their authors to have an agent's representation, and then work on a new book you hope your agent will shop, or (d) stick with your agent, shelve the book because you trust your agent when they tell you something's not working with the story, and start working on something new.

Matters of money and accounting should also be laid out in the agency agreement. Look for how payments will be remitted to you, how long the agent will take to process payments once they've received your earnings from your publisher (no more than ten business days is the current requirement for agents who are members of the Association of Authors' Representatives), and what documentation the agent will provide along with your payments.

And let's not forget the little matter of your agent's commission. For domestic publishing deals, an agent's standard commission is 15%. For subrights deals like translation or film/TV, which often require the involvement of a co-agent who specializes in placing those rights, the commissions will vary territory to territory and deal to deal. Look for anything from 15% to 25% commissions there.

Other financial considerations you might see in an agency agreement include which expenses the agent may incur on your behalf, and which may be charged back to you—things like photocopying, printing, postage, and shipping. This was a bigger deal back in the days before digital, when your manuscript had to be printed and shipped out to editors. Nowadays, charge-back expenses might include the cost of extra copies of your book that your agent will send out to film/TV and foreign-rights co-agents, translators, reviewers, etc.

What agents *can't* charge back to you are things like office supplies, rent, utilities, or other operating costs or general overhead expenses.

A few other agent rights you might see in an agency agreement include:

- The agent's right to represent other authors who write in your genre(s) or for your target audience, which is not to be considered a conflict of the agent's interests or yours.
- The agent's right to have a standard agency clause included in all contracts they negotiate on your behalf. The agency clause exists to make your agent's stake in the publishing agreement official and legally binding.
- The agent's right to work with co-agents on your behalf.

Some additional author rights stipulated in the agreement might include:

- The author's right to review and approve or reject all material changes the agent wishes to make to the author's material.
- The author's right to hold the copyrights to all their works.
- The author's right, in the event of the agent's death, to gain control of all their intellectual property and related future earnings. In other words, if your agent dies, you're on your own, responsible for handling all matters related to

all existing deals and free to assign the handling of such existing deals to a new agent. In other words, your agent can't bequeath your rights, whether sold or unsold, or their commission on your future earnings to their estate.

Finally, you'll most likely see a clause in the agreement stipulating that both the agent and author agree to participate in arbitration should they ever hit a legal snag. But let's hope that never happens!

STEP 9

AGENT REVISIONS

ONCE YOU'VE BOTH PUT YOUR SIGNATURES ON THE agency agreement, you're off to the races. Right?

Maybe not quite yet. As already mentioned in Step 7 (offer of representation), your agent will probably want to work with you through at least one round of revisions before they put your manuscript out on submission.

Why? Aren't writers supposed to get their manuscripts as close to perfect as they can before they start querying agents?

Yes, they are! But the difference here is that agents have their fingers on the pulse of the industry. They know what's working with editors at any given time—and what isn't. Therefore, an agent's editorial pass will be done with an eye toward improving your manuscript not only *storywise* and *craftwise*, but also *marketwise*.

And therein lies the value of landing an editorially minded agent.

Not all agents are equally editorially minded. Some agents don't edit much at all, preferring instead to operate on a quick-turnaround basis or a throw-a-bunch-of-stuff-out-there-and-see-what-sticks model. Sign a new client today, submit their manuscript tomorrow. Lather. Rinse. Repeat.

Any agent who works this way—sign, sign, sign, submit, submit, submit—is bound to make a few sales. Some make a lot of sales. But what happens to their author-clients whose books don't sell? "I'm sorry this one didn't work out," these agents might say. "Let me know when your next book is ready and we'll try again."

That leaves you, the author, adrift once again.

Agents who are more editorially minded are perhaps working toward a few major sales with lots of subrights potential rather than lots of little ones for niche markets or readerships. Editorially minded agents keep their client lists shorter so they can spend more time and effort developing each client's projects and supporting each client's career. They work with their authors closely on each book because they are attaching their professional name and reputation to each book, so they want it to be as awesome as possible before they send it out.

STEP 10

SUBMISSION

ONCE YOUR MANUSCRIPT IS READY TO SUBMIT TO acquiring editors, it's time for you and your agent to discuss submission strategy. At this point, the two of you might be working on a new title for the book. You might be doing a little market research and fine-tuning your list of comparable titles. You'll definitely be polishing your pitch, starting with that awesome pitch you will already have written for your query letter. If your agent wants to go after a two- or three-book deal, you might even be writing pitches for subsequent books, whether you planned to write subsequent books or not. (Welcome to the business!)

Then your agent will share their list of top-tier editors with you, and out your book will go.

Now for more waiting. Hopefully, the wait won't be too long, but sometimes it can drag on for months. Remember to keep writing during these long stretches of waiting!

If none of the editors on your agent's top-tier list wants to buy your book, a couple of different things might happen. First, you have the right to read editors' rejections, so if your agent hasn't already forwarded them to you as a matter of course, ask that they send them along.

Editors' rejections run the gamut from short and sweet to in-depth and detailed. But in general, you'll get more feedback about your book from editors at this stage of the game than you did from agents back when you were querying.

Best case, you and your agent will find a common thread in editors' rejections—something concrete you can address, with your agent's help, in another round of revisions. Maybe that issue is craft related. Maybe these editors all commented that they found your main character unlikeable or unrelatable, or maybe they pointed out that your main character didn't really change much as a result of your story's events. Maybe they all commented that your story got off to a slow start (writers do, time and time again, tend to frontload their books with exposition and backstory, which is *extremely* difficult to do well.) Or maybe your story logic fell apart at a particular point; your plot spun off in a weird direction; your story world wasn't as well developed as it could have been; your conflicts were too easily resolved; or some element of your story was simply implausible, asking the reader for too much suspension of disbelief. The list goes on.

Maybe, on the other hand, the issue is market related. Editors might love your writing and story execution, but your book might be so different, so unusual, that they can't pin down who your readers would be. Maybe you wrote a genre-bender or a cross-genre novel…but you bent the genre a little too far, or you crossed genres in such a way that editors can't see it selling well to either genre's established readership. Or maybe, on the other hand, you've written to a trend or established trope that's already in decline. Vampires. Dystopias. Pirates. Fairytale retellings. Sexy handymen. This list goes on, too, though it's shiftier and more difficult to predict. Whatever the case, if an editor is unsure how your book would be positioned in bookstores or libraries—if they could even sell it to bookstore and library buyers in the first place—then they are unlikely to make you an offer.

More frustrating, though, is when ten editors turn down your book, and you're left with ten very different reasons why. Where do you go from there?

Regardless of whether or not editors' rejections gave you something concrete to work with, you and your agent will have to decide what to do next. Either you'll pull the book back and retool it, or you'll send it out to another round of editors.

Keep in mind that publishing houses regularly run profit-and-loss statements on each of their editors. *That means editors have to generate profit if they want to continue being employed.* And that means that in any given fiscal quarter, editors are balancing their acquisitions of solid bets with their acquisitions of riskier titles. Solid bets are books whose sales editors can predict because they are by known authors with established reader bases, or they are books by debut authors that deliver something the editor knows will resonate with a comparable title's audience or author's established reader base. Riskier books, on the other hand, are often by unknown writers; they break known molds and will either totally flop with readers or take off and become runaway bestsellers. Every editor is different, with a different risk tolerance, so I can't speak to how *all* editors strike that balance. But I'm guessing it's not fifty/fifty. It's probably something closer to seventy/thirty or even eighty/twenty (solid bets/risks).

Knowing this, and putting yourself in the shoes of an editor striving to keep their P&L sheet in the black, you can see why it might be easier for new writers to break into traditional publishing if they write squarely in a particular genre, delivering the favored tropes of that genre's audience (in a new or unique way, of course!). So one strategy for writers hoping to land a traditional-publishing deal is to write inside the established boundaries of a particular genre to break in, and then, once established, either continue to write in that genre or begin to write outside it.

Now, that's not a strategy that will work for or appeal to every writer. And that's OK. None of this is to say that a debut author can't break big with an off-center, genre-busting novel. In fact, such things happen all the time. After all, every editor dreams of being the one to discover the next J. K. Rowling, and they can't do that without taking a chance on something once in a while that doesn't fit inside a familiar, comfortable box.

Just know what type of writer you are and what risks you're willing to take. Know that every writer, based on what they write and what their short- and long-term goals are, will face different challenges and find different in-roads to traditional publishing.

STEP 11

OFFER OF PUBLICATION

In a perfect world, every editor who reads your manuscript will want to buy it.

In a more realistic but still pretty darn-good world, you'll get some rejections, but you'll draw the eye of more than one editor. This might lead to an auction. Very exciting!

Different agents run auctions in different ways, which I won't go into in great detail here. But in general, your agent will set some parameters for the editors who are throwing their hats in the ring—anything from which rights, subrights, and territories are on the table (and, more importantly, which aren't) to the minimum advance that will be considered.

Some editors might drop out at this point. Those who

agree to the parameters submit their offers to your agent, blind to the bids of the other editors still in the game. This might be a best-bids auction, in which editors have only one shot at making an offer, or a round-robin auction, in which the agent allows each editor two or three tries to woo the author. Editors might sweeten their offers by, for example:

- Allowing the agent to retain particular rights on the author's behalf, like audio or translation rights.
- Offering for two or three books instead of one.
- Offering royalties escalators. (See Step 15 for more information on royalties.)
- Providing attractive bonus clauses.
- Pledging to pay your advance all at once or in two increments instead of three, four, or even more increments. (We'll talk more about advances on the next page.)
- Expediting publication—say, twelve months or less as opposed to the more common eighteen to twenty-four months from the date of the contract.
- Committing to publishing the book in both hardcover and trade paperback, or to publishing a special edition.
- Writing special marketing efforts into the contract, like making the book a lead title in the

publisher's catalogue for the particular season in which it will be published or giving it prime exposure at major industry and trade events.

Your agent will then share the editors' bids with you and talk you through the pros and cons of each. Rarely will you be comparing apples to apples. The important thing to note is that the bid that contains the highest advance—which is, naturally, the first place a writer's eyes go—is only sometimes the best overall offer.

So let's take a minute here to talk about advances.

Whatever advance you are offered, rarely will it be paid out to you all at once. Advances are often paid out to the author a bit at a time at particular steps along the way. Typical steps include when you sign your contract (called the on-signing payment), when you deliver an editorially acceptable manuscript (called the delivery-and-acceptance or D&A payment), when your initial edition is officially published (called the on-publication payment), and when subsequent editions are published, such as the trade paperback or mass-market paperback editions. Yet another increment that newer, untested authors might see on a multi-book contract is the D&A of an outline. That might be because your editor wants to make sure you've thought all the way through your story ideas for your future books before you go through the trouble of writing the manuscripts, or it might be because the publisher is just looking for another opportunity to further apportion your total advance. Typically, the larger the advance, the harder the publisher is going to push to pay you out in more increments over a greater period of time. Let's look at an example.

Say you get an offer from Fancy Publishing House for three books at $25,000 per book. That means your total advance will be $75,000. Yay! You immediately start typing your resignation letter. Time to quit your day job!

But wait.

There are dozens of ways your publisher could offer to structure the payout of your $75,000 advance. Here's one:

- For Book I, one-fourth on signing: $6,250
- For Book I, one-fourth on D&A: $6,250
- For Book I, one-fourth on publication of the hardcover edition (eighteen months from signing of contract): $6,250
- For Book I, one-fourth on publication of the trade-paperback edition, or twelve months following the publication of the hardcover edition, whichever comes first: $6,250
- For Book II, one-fifth on signing: $5,000
- For Book II, one-fifth on D&A of outline: $5,000
- For Book II, one-fifth on D&A of manuscript (to be delivered no more than twelve months after the D&A of the manuscript for Book I): $5,000

- For Book II, one-fifth on publication of the hardcover edition (twelve months following publication of the hardcover edition of Book I): $5,000
- For Book II, one-fifth on publication of the trade-paperback edition, or twelve months following the publication of the hardcover edition of Book II, whichever comes first: $5,000
- For Book III, one-fifth on signing: $5,000
- For Book III, one-fifth on D&A of outline: $5,000
- For Book III, one-fifth on D&A of manuscript (to be delivered no more than twelve months after the D&A of the manuscript for Book II): $5,000
- For Book III, one-fifth on publication of the hardcover edition (twelve months following publication of the hardcover edition of Book II): $5,000
- For Book III, one-fifth on publication of the trade-paperback edition, or twelve months following the publication of the hardcover edition of Book III, whichever comes first: $5,000

So how much money are you going to get and when? Well, let's say you sign your contract in July 2019 and deliver the manuscript for Book I the same day. As long as you make all your deadlines for your outlines and manuscripts, here's how you can expect to be paid:

- **In 2019, you'll receive $27,500.**
  - July 2019: $22,500 (on signing for all three books plus D&A for Book I).
  - August 2019: $5,000 (on D&A of outline for Book II)
- **In 2020, you'll receive $10,000.**
  - July 2020: $5,000 (on D&A of manuscript for Book II).
  - August 2020: $5,000 (on D&A of outline for Book III)
- **In 2021, you'll receive $11,250.**
  - January 2021: $6,250 (on publication of hardcover of Book I)
  - July 2021: $5,000 (on D&A of manuscript for Book III)
- **In 2022, you'll receive $11,250.**
  - January 2022: $11,250 (on publication of trade paperback of Book I and hardcover of Book II).
- **In 2023, you'll receive $10,000.**
  - January 2023: $10,000 (on publication of the trade paperback of Book II and hardcover edition of Book III)
- **In 2024, you'll receive $5,000.**
  - January 2024: $5,000 (on publication of trade paperback edition of Book III)

Still think it's wise to quit your day job? Maybe. Maybe not. The point is, payment schedules can be complicated, and they may or may not be compatible with the lifestyle you were hoping to achieve.

That said, every deal is different. A much simpler payout schedule for a debut author being offered a modest advance for a one-book deal would be half of the advance on signing and half on publication (which can be anywhere from twelve to twenty-four months later).

In the end, the thing to keep in mind is that not only the amount of the advance, but also how it will be apportioned and paid out are all subject to negotiation.

Now that you have a better sense of how advances can play into publication offers, let's get back to our auction scenario…

Once you have all the bids in front of you, your agent might set up conference calls so that you can get to know each of the editors vying for your book. Once again, as you did before signing with your agent, you'll be listening to others' editorial vision of your work and thinking about whose vision most closely meshes with yours. (Yes, there's another round of revisions coming.)

Auctions aren't super common, so if your book ends up at the center of one, that's cause to celebrate.

Another cool way your book might sell is called a pre-empt. That's when an editor stays up all night reading your manuscript, calls your agent at four in the morning because they can't wait any longer, and leaves a message that says, "This book must be mine. I'll make you a sweet offer if you pull it off all the other editors' desks."

This puts you and your agent in a great position for negotiating. After your agent gets the offer in writing, there are several different directions you could go.

- Your agent might advise you to accept the pre-empt.
- Your agent might look at the "sweet offer" the editor put together and tell you it's not nearly as sweet as it needs to be. In this case, your agent might let the editor know how the deal needs to improve before they will consider accepting the pre-empt and pulling the manuscript off submission.
- Your agent might leverage the pre-empt to drum up an auction. They'll call all the other editors they submitted your manuscript to and say, "Are you in or out? Let me know by Friday."

Whichever way your pre-empt goes, it's always nice to know that an editor loved your work that much—even if that's not the editor who ultimately lands your book.

However, know that few books are sold in auctions or pre-empts. Most deals are done pretty simply, with a lot of rejections and one offer of acquisition/publication.

And that's cause to celebrate, too. Once you've received an offer that you are happy to accept, from an editor that you are excited to work with, you and your agent are ready to put the deal in motion.

STEP 12

DEAL AND CONTRACT NEGOTIATION

THE NEXT STEP IS THAT YOUR AGENT AND YOUR NEW editor will negotiate the deal points—the major, top-level terms that each party (publisher and author) will be giving to and receiving from the other...as well as which terms each party will *not* be giving to or receiving from the other.

These deal points will be written up on a deal memo, a one- or two-page document that your agent and editor should both sign off on *in writing* before moving to the contracts stage.

I can't count how many negotiations have been streamlined, how many misunderstandings easily cleared up, how many contentious arguments prevented, simply because our agents insist that editors sign the deal memo. Never assume that verbal agreement is going to be remembered or honored when it comes to hashing out a publishing contract!

The deal memo is then passed to the publisher's contracts department, where someone plugs the deal points into the appropriate clauses in the publisher's boilerplate contract.

Finally, the contract is combed over by the agent, and the finer points of it are negotiated further. The contract might pass back and forth between the agent and the contracts person several times, and it might take several months before the contract is agreeable to both parties.

Be very wary if your agent doesn't appear to have negotiated much, because you should never sign the publisher's boilerplate contract. What should tip you off is a super-speedy turnaround time. A solid, well-negotiated contract takes time to prepare.

Once your agent sends you your contract to sign, ask them to send you a copy of the original, un-negotiated contract so that you can compare it to the version they're asking you to sign. Also ask them for the deal memo, and make sure all the deal points are properly represented in the final contract.

Ideally, you shouldn't have to do this. Ideally, you'd trust your agent to do this part of their job on your behalf. But at the end of the day, it's your signature that's getting inked on the dotted line, not theirs. It's your responsibility to know what you're signing. And it's your responsibility to hold your agent accountable. At the end of the day, *you're* paying *them* to perform a highly specialized service. *Caveat emptor.*

I know writers who, even though they have an agent, pay intellectual property attorneys thousands of dollars to review their contracts because "contracts aren't my agent's strong suit." That makes me sad. However, just as there are agents who are editorially minded and agents who aren't, and just as there are agents who are strongly business-minded and agents who aren't, there are agents who are contract savvy…and agents who aren't.

Yes, some agents understand contracts and how to negotiate them. Others don't. If you're realizing you signed with the latter type of agent, then think about how you're benefitting from that relationship and whether it's worth the 15% commission you're paying them. If you're not paying them to negotiate on your behalf, then I hope they're earning their commission doing other things for you that you couldn't do on your own.

OK. Let's get back to the deal-negotiation piece for a minute.

If the deal is the result of an auction, and if your agent was very clear up front with the editors who participated in that auction regarding what rights, territories, and other deal parameters were and were not on the table, then there shouldn't be any surprises during the deal negotiation. But sometimes there are.

If an agent isn't perfectly crystal-clear up front, that leaves room for the editor who won the auction to say things during the negotiation like, "It was my understanding I was bidding for world rights, not world English; otherwise, I never would have offered an advance that high." Or, "Here at [Big Five Publisher], we never do deals where audio rights aren't included. You know that about us, so that should have been assumed as a matter of course when I entered the auction." Or, "For an advance this size, we're going to have to insist on paying out in fourths."

This is where it begins to pay off for you that you chose an agent who stands their ground and isn't afraid to negotiate. The last thing you want or need is a super-nice agent who backs down and folds the minute a negotiation starts because they lack the business savvy to push back, because they're afraid to get tough, or because they worry that people won't like them.

Remember: It's not your agent's job to be liked. It's your agent's job to *do their job,* which is to negotiate *for you,* in *your best interests.* Your publishing house, especially if it's Big Five, will have an entire team of contracts people lined up behind your editor, and those negotiators have zero emotional connection to your manuscript. They don't care about it the way your editor does. Their job is to make the best possible deal happen *for their publishing house,* even if they insist on terms that ultimately kill the deal before it happens.

So you need an agent who can respond to these kinds of negotiation tactics with, "No, I was quite clear before the auction—*and here's proof in writing*—that world rights were never on the table." Or, "Actually, you *do* allow the author to retain audio rights on certain deals. Here are two contracts we did with you earlier this year in which you allowed the author to retain audio." Or, "The advance isn't *that* big. Look. In the past, you've paid out much larger advances in halves or thirds, not fourths."

Your agent knows what terms they can get during the deal-points negotiation. They know what to ask for, how to make a case for getting it, and how hard to push. They also know what's reasonable to bend on, because, after all, the ideal deal must end up being mutually beneficial.

Your agent also knows when to walk away from a deal. Know that deals do fall apart at the negotiation stage. It's rare, but it happens. It's like calling off the wedding at the rehearsal dinner—heartbreaking, and you have to give all the presents back, but everyone is going to survive.

If your agent encourages you to walk away from a deal,

here's what you need to know. The reason is most likely that whomever they are negotiating with at the publishing house, whether it's the editor or someone in the contracts department, isn't budging on some contractual term or another that (a) damages your career or is blatantly unfair to you, or (b) sets a dangerous precedent for the agent or agency, for agents at large, and, by extension, for writers at large.

Either situation is a bitter pill for you, the author, to swallow.

If the negotiation is stalling out because of (a), unfair terms, the hope is that continued negotiation can iron out the wrinkle. This might happen only after one party has declared they're walking away. Maybe it's a bluff. Maybe not. But it might bring the *agent* back to the negotiating table with something like, "OK, I understand you won't allow us to retain audio rights. So how about you agree to revert the rights to the author after one year if during that time you haven't published an audio edition?" Or, "OK, I understand you can't go any higher on the advance. How about you bump up the royalties or give us a bonus clause?" Likewise, it might bring the *publisher* back with something like, "OK, I understand that it's important for you to retain translation rights for this project, so will you accept a slightly lower advance?" Or, "OK, we'll raise the out-of-print threshold if you agree to…" Negotiation is give and take. You get the idea.

If, however, the negotiation is stalling out because of (b), setting a dangerous precedent, well, that's tougher for writers to understand. So let me explain.

Imagine feeding a toddler cake and ice cream for dinner every night for a week. Then on the eighth night, you set a plate of broccoli before them. How's that going to end up for you? Not great.

An agent who gives in a lot—who has a habit of feeding a publisher lots of yummy cake and ice cream on behalf of their clients—is going to have a tough time getting that publisher to eat broccoli on *your* behalf.

Every publishing deal is built on the deals that came before it, so if an agent gives in on a particular deal point *even just this once*, then it will be that much harder for that agent to make a case that the publisher should grant them that deal point in future negotiations.

Yes, there is a magical phrase that appears in a lot of publishing contracts: *not to be deemed a precedent*. This can be tacked onto any clause either added to or stricken from the boilerplate by either the agent or the publisher. Its intent is to keep that special-case clause from coming back to bite future deals. But the truth is, both parties know that if the other agreed to budge on that particular point *now*, then they might agree to budge on it again *later*. So it's going to come up. Anything your agent doesn't hold firm on is fair game in future negotiations with that publisher.

Therefore, anytime a publisher won't give on something that the agent knows is reasonable and in the best interest of all authors—not just *you*, the author at the center of *this* negotiation, but *all authors*—then the agent might choose to walk away from the deal.

That's a huge bummer for you. I get it. That makes you a sacrificial lamb. Why should *your* deal fall apart so your agent can maybe get better deals for other authors in the future? Why should *your* book not make it to bookstore shelves just because your agent is being a stubborn negotiator?

There are no easy answers. Worst case, you insist you want to go forward with the deal, despite the unfavorable or damaging terms insisted on by your publisher. Why would you do this? Because you're a writer, and the only thing you've ever wanted is to see your published book on bookstore shelves—a worthy dream, but one that has blinded many a writer to career-injuring legal consequences. In this case, your agent might sever your relationship, unwilling as they are to give in to injurious terms, and you might have to find another agent right quick before your publisher kills the deal. Remember that most Big Five publishers don't negotiate deals with unagented authors, so no agent, no deal.

Another outcome might be that your agent advises you to walk away, and you agree. The deal dies, and you go back out on submission again, to another round of editors.

This all probably sounds very doom-and-gloom. In truth, these are worst-case scenarios, and it's valuable for writers caught up in the publishing machine to know and understand the wide range of situations that can befall them, and *why* they happen.

However, it's also valuable for writers to know that most publishing deals are going to go through just fine because, at the end of the day, your editor, who is your champion inside your publishing house, *wants your book*. They believe that your book is a valuable property, that it's going to add gains to their P&L sheet, and they want to partner with you. Most negotiations proceed in good faith, with both parties invested in ultimately arriving at the place of mutual benefit.

STEP 13

MARKETING AND PROMOTION

YOU'LL BE PUTTING PLENTY OF MARKETING AND promotion efforts into your book *after* it's published, but a great deal of those efforts will happen now, to set your book up for a successful launch.

I know that marketing and promotion are a big concern among writers, published and pre-published alike. My aim here is not to give you strategies for marketing your book, but to dispel some myths and provide you with some basic insight into how marketing decisions get made.

As you approach your publication date, you, your agent, and your editor will start strategizing. If your publisher has a marketing and publicity department (the Big Five and their imprints do), then your agent will invite a member of that department to join in on those conversations. Or the publisher will already have assigned an in-house marketing pro to you and your book. These conversations will be focused on the questions *Who are our readers?* and *What are the best and most cost- and effort-effective ways to get this book into their hands?*

At conferences, I hear a lot of writers decrying publishers' marketing efforts. Among the most common declarations I hear from published writers are:

- "My book bombed because my publisher didn't do anything to promote it."
- "All my publisher did to market my book was…"
- "My book did OK, but that's only because I paid for all my own marketing and promotion."

This kind of anecdotal rhetoric turns into the following generalizations, which get passed around writer tribes, often with an air of alarm:

- "Publishers won't pay a single dime to promote your book!"
- "Publishers don't even *have* marketing budgets!"
- "I hear that once I get published, I'm on my own. Am I really going to have to do all my own marketing? How much is that going to cost me?"

First of all, publishers *do* have marketing budgets. Of course they do. And many publishing houses employ professionals whose full-time job it is to get their books into the hands of paying customers. Some even employ marketing pros whose sole job is to promote the publisher's backlist titles—books that have been on bookstore shelves longer than a year but that have (with proper promotion) long shelf-lives ahead of them.

Does that mean publishers have unlimited resources? No. Does it mean that every book they publish is going to get an equal slice of their marketing pie? No. Just as I mentioned earlier regarding publishers' efforts to sell subrights, publishers must make decisions about how to best maximize their return on the marketing dollars they spend.

How does that work? Let's take a look. If Publisher A plans to publish twenty books next fall, they will make data-driven predictions about which of those twenty books will break big with readers. So the publisher might pick three, maybe four of the twenty to be their frontlist titles—books that will be most competitive in the market because they have the greatest potential to generate buzz among booksellers, librarians, schools, book clubs, awards committees, and media outlets (TV, radio, newspapers, magazines), which are always hungry to cover the Next Big Thing and the Hot New Author. Maybe a book is made frontlist simply because the author is a perennial bestseller, like Stephen King or Jodi Picoult. Or maybe a book by a debut novelist gets picked because it's timely or so groundbreakingly unique or beautiful that everyone on the publisher's team is invested in making sure it's an immediate hit among readers.

At the end of the day, more resources will be allocated to frontlist titles because it makes good business sense to boost those titles up as high as possible into the competitive space. Put differently, the three or four books Publisher A chooses to spotlight next fall will most likely generate more profit than all sixteen or seventeen of the quieter, lower-profile books they are also publishing combined.

So will you, as the author, once you're published, have to invest some time and effort in marketing and promotion? Yes, if you want you want to build a solid readership who will vociferously demand more books from you, which means more contracts in your future. Again, you are your books' best and most enthusiastic advocate, so why wouldn't you invest in marketing? I imagine you introverts are sinking deeper into your couch cushions as you read this, but hopefully your agent as well as a marketing or publicity pro from your publisher's team will provide some coaching and strategies.

As an author, will you be able to measure the success of your time and efforts by seeing corelative unit sales or earnings? Not really. A lot of marketing and promotion is a bit of a shot in the dark. Your team writes press releases and sends them to magazines, newspapers, and radio stations. They send uncorrected proofs—also known as galleys or advance reader copies (ARCs)—to the big national reviewers (*Publishers Weekly*, *Kirkus*, *Library Journal*, NPR, *The New York Times*, etc.) as well as genre-specific reviewers and book bloggers. You talk to other authors and find out what's working for them. You think about whether it can work for you, too—for your readers and your genre. You do your best to construct campaigns that will connect your book with the widest sector of its intended audience. You're active on social media. You put out a monthly e-newsletter. You do the blog tours and the bookstore signings and the school visits and the author interviews with your city's local magazine. You teach workshops at conferences and sit on panels at conventions and give talks at your local library. Basically, you sow seeds. And maybe you see a little sales growth here and there, but rarely will you really know for sure which seeds sprouted that growth. That can be frustrating.

Instead of thinking of these tasks as chores or necessary evils, think of them simply as best practices. They bring you face-to-face with readers and establish your voice, authority, and brand in the book world. Once you are a published author, these duties are simply a part of the professional writer's life.

What about a budget? How much money will you

have to spend to participate in these sorts of promotional activities? There's no good answer for that. Start by getting yourself a good accountant who can advise you on such things, and in the meantime, save your receipts. Most promotion-related expenses, including those for traveling to and from events where you are actively selling your book or building your brand, are tax deductible.

On this topic, I'll share a quick anecdote. Several years ago, one of our clients whose debut book was soon to be released by a Big Five publisher invested something like ten-thousand dollars of their own money on marketing and publicity. The book enjoyed a highly successful release, and sales continued to be robust for years after the book's initial publication. Yay for this author!

However: Can we 100% positively corelate any of that up-front cash with the book's sales or success? Not really. Would the book have been successful anyway without the author's having put up so much of their own money? We'll never know for sure. But the author did make back that money and then some (and then *a lot*, actually), so it turned out to be a good gamble. It was a gutsy move that paid off.

Does this mean you should put thousands of dollars into your own marketing? Does it mean that if you don't, your book will automatically be on the one-way street to Failure Town? No. But please don't launch your own campaign blindly, throwing money at the proverbial wall to see what might stick—especially if you don't have a background in marketing or a solid grasp of how the readers of your particular genre think when they're making book-buying decisions. I tell you this story only to remark that any money put forth to promote a book, whether it's yours or your publisher's, will most likely generate at least some return. Some writers will make back their initial investments. Some won't.

In general, it takes money to make money. This we know. We also know that books with no promotional support typically perform poorly in market. There are always outliers, of course: we've all heard that one writer on that one panel at that one conference who boisterously proclaims, "Neither I nor my publisher spent a single red cent on promotion, but my book sold a bazillion copies and I am now fabulously wealthy!"

Of course we all want to be that person, but don't go into this industry *planning* or *expecting* to be that person. Go in with your eyes open, expecting that like ninety-nine percent of writers just like you, you're going to have to roll up your sleeves and dig in. More often than not, hard work, persistence, and willingness to risk trying new things trumps luck.

Now, I mentioned earlier that it's difficult for authors to correlate which of their promotional efforts yielded results in terms of sales or earnings. However, that's not the same story for marketing professionals who work in larger publishing houses. That's because, over the years or decades they've been in business, they've launched thousands of books to millions of readers—most likely, depending on the imprint, all of a known demographic who read a particular genre. Pros can predict with far more accuracy which efforts will maximize sales for a given book because they have the benefit of being in possession of a vast data set that you, Debut Author with First Novel, just don't have. Therefore, if the idea of marketing your book stresses you out, then make it a point at your next writers conference to attend the breakout sessions on marketing—but understand that you're going to get totally different insights if those sessions are taught by marketing professionals with in-house experience at a large publishing house than you will if those sessions are taught by writers, whether published traditionally or independently. The marketing insights you'll get from other writers are typically of the "here's what worked for me" and "here are some things I've heard work for other writers too" variety. These strategies may or may not translate successfully to your genre or readership.

Plus, any marketing strategy that worked yesterday can be rendered obsolete today, given how often a certain Online Bookselling Giant changes the algorithms that dictate how books are discovered, i.e., which books pop up at the top of the screen when readers search for their next read. (Hint: The top books are often titles published by the Online Bookselling Giant's own publishing imprints.) The Giant also has a history of frequently changing how publishers' cuts and authors' earnings are calculated. Frustrating to be sure, and completely out of your control, so you can either tune out the noise and trust that your agent and publisher are doing their jobs on your behalf, or you can stay abreast of such things, as plenty of savvy writers do, and be more active in marketing your book.

There's no right answer. Choose the path that you have the most brain space for and that won't stop you from taking joy in writing books. In this ever-changing industry, that is the only constant.

STEP 14

PUBLICATION

PUBLICATION WILL TYPICALLY HAPPEN TWELVE TO twenty-four months following the signing of the contract. Eighteen months is fairly standard, and any additional books on a multi-book contract will probably be scheduled for publication every twelve months afterward.

What happens during those months leading up to the release of your first book?

You'll be working closely with your editor on yet another round of revisions. This means your editor is going to send you an editorial letter. Maybe you'll get your letter right after your contract is signed because your editor has been working on your book at the same time her contracts person has been working with your agent to hammer out your contract. Or maybe you'll get your letter in a few weeks because your editor waited until your contract was signed to get started.

Your editorial letter might be on the light side—a page or so with a bulleted list of little tweaks. Or it might be on the heavy side. Maybe you need to cut 20,000 words, develop one of your characters more deeply, weave in a new subplot, or completely retool the mushy middle or the third act.

Whatever the case, once you receive your editorial letter, you'll probably be given no more than a few weeks to address your editor's concerns and return the revised manuscript.

Welcome to being a professional writer on deadline.

You're in the publication pipeline now, rolling downhill toward your release date. There's no extra time built into your publisher's schedule, or your editor's, for you to freeze up or overthink. In fact, your editor is probably working on dozens of books at any given time. Maybe more. (One well-known, award-winning Big Five editor recently mentioned on a panel at a conference that she is sometimes working on as many as fifty books at a time, all with deadlines of their own.) So if you don't make *your* deadline, you're on the path to damaging your relationship with your editor...and along with it, your professional reputation.

No matter what, strive to make your deadlines.

After you turn in your revised manuscript, it will go into copyediting. When your editor sends you the copyedited manuscript, you'll have to drop everything to review it and turn it in on time. Then not long after that, you'll get the typeset manuscript to proofread—at which point you can't make any changes other than to correct glaring errors.

If you're under a two- or three-book contract, all this gets even more challenging. How? Imagine trying to write Book II (which you now have mere months to complete and turn in) when you receive your edit letter for Book I. Not only does your creative headspace start swinging like a pendulum between the two stories, but your momentum on Book II keeps stalling out because your editor needs you to comb through Book I yet again. Which is making you cross-eyed because it's starting to look like nothing more to you than a jumble of complete nonsense. By the time Book I comes out, you'll be so sick of it that when a reader approaches you at your first book-signing event to smugly point out a typo on page two, you'll be ready to pack in the whole professional writing thing.

Hopefully you don't pack it in. After all, for most, becoming a published author is the realization of a lifelong dream, despite the minutiae of getting the book ready!

Your publication date will depend on several factors. Publishers plan their catalogs carefully, not only in terms of how many books they can publish in a particular season, but also in terms of variety and timeliness. For instance, two books that happen to be based on a similar premise will most likely be scheduled for publication in different seasons. Or if Publisher A finds out Publisher B is releasing a book similar to one on their own list scheduled to hit the market in the same season, then Publisher A might either rush to get their book out first or delay their book's publication to avoid the possibility that it will be overshadowed by Publisher B's book. A novel that explores some unique "what if" question may get moved up on the publisher's schedule if a big current event occurs that just so happens to put that particular "what if" to the test. Or, depending on a novel's subject, its publication may be scheduled to coincide with a major occasion that's expected to make a massive impression on the public's imagination—for example, the Olympic Games, a landmark election, a total solar eclipse, or an important historical anniversary.

A big bummer is when your book's release date gets pushed back because the publisher decides, for whatever reason, to swap it out with something they want to publish sooner. Not much you can do about that but be gracious, be patient, and keep writing. However, not every pubdate push-back is a bad thing. You might receive news that your release date is being delayed a few months because the publisher decided to give your book a big, splashy release at a major trade or library event. Imagine thirty-foot-tall banners of your book cover towering over the show floor. In that type of situation, waiting a few extra months for the release will definitely be worth your while, both for building your brand and maximizing your sales.

Regardless of the publication schedule stipulated in your contract, your publisher may shift you around. A good agent will stay on top of such shifts, though, and if you get shifted more than once, they'll put up a fight. And win. You want to see your book available for sale, and a good agent makes sure it happens. After all, they don't get paid until you get paid.

ROYALTIES AND ACCOUNTING

THE DAY YOU RECEIVE THE ENVELOPE CONTAINING YOUR first royalty statement—hopefully along with a check!—is pretty exciting. But then you tear open the envelope and look at the statement…and confusion ensues.

Before we dive into this rather complex topic, let me just say that I'm going to do my best to make royalties as easy to understand as possible; however, if you find that your eyes are starting to cross, or if you begin to weep openly or gnash your teeth, let me re-emphasize the point I made earlier about asking your agent if they, or someone they employ, will audit, or help you audit, your royalty statements. Getting the support you need to ensure correct accounting is one of the best things you can do to advocate for yourself as a professional writer.

After years of auditing royalty statements on behalf of the clients at Nelson Literary Agency, I can tell you that the Big Five publishers produce clean, easy-to-read-and-understand statements. Each of the Big Five's statements are formatted differently, but once you know what you're looking at, you can see that all the information you'd expect to find on a royalty statement is there, and most of the time, the numbers check out down to the penny. (But not all the time. Mistakes get made. I'll get into that later.) That's because the Big Five have fully staffed accounting departments—*numbers* people among a sea of *words* people. This is a good thing, for them and for you.

I can also tell you that if you publish with a small or mid-sized press, your royalty statements might be pretty good. Or they might be complete garbage. You might get an email with an attached Excel spreadsheet containing a couple rows of numbers and dubious, incorrect, broken, or missing formulas. Or you might get no royalty statements at all, despite what your contract says or how often your agent calls your publisher and threatens to report them to the AAR, *Publishers Weekly*, and other industry watchdogs for their failure to report or pay.

When it comes to publishers' accounting practices, I've seen the good, the bad, the ugly…and the downright nefarious.

Again, learning to audit your own royalty statements is a best practice. To that end, here are some things you should know about royalties.

ROYALTIES SCHEDULES

Most Big Five publishers prepare royalty statements twice per year. They will send your statements to your agent, and your agent will then forward your statements to you, along with payment, if payment is due. You will receive the amount on your statement minus your agent's commission.

The vast majority of Big Five publishers divide their year into two accounting periods: January 1 to June 30, and July 1 to December 31. Publishers then have three months following the end of each accounting period to prepare all their authors' statements and remit payment. That means that every October and April, literary agencies get slammed by a deluge of their clients' royalty statements, which need to be downloaded, scanned, saved, sent out, reviewed, and, if necessary, questioned. Some Big Five books, however, end up on different semiannual accounting schedules, so those royalty statements come not in April/October, but in December/June, January/July, February/August, March/September, or May/November.

Other publishers, like Audible and Harlequin, provide quarterly statements, currently in February, May, August, and November. A few smaller publishers report monthly.

Some Big Five still send their statements to agents via snail mail, but most have gone paperless. They maintain online portals where agents can go to download and save royalty statements, and then forward them to their authors. (By the way, these publishers also provide author portals, where authors can log in at any time and see their books' most up-to-date sales figures, subrights sales, etc.) At Nelson Literary Agency, we maintain online portals for each of our clients, so every period, instead of emailing our clients' statements, we drop them in their portals.

Note that your contract will include an accounting clause that clearly states when and how often your publisher must send you a statement. If they do not adhere to that schedule, then they are in breach of contract. This is another situation in which having a tough agent will come in handy. A tough agent isn't afraid to be assertive with small or mid-sized publishers who are "too busy" to get their statements out on time or who keep promising that their statements will arrive "in a week or two," yet in a week or two…nothing.

We deal with this kind of thing from small and mid-sized publishers more often than we should have to. Sad but true. In my royalties-auditing experience, I've had to call folks at any number of these non-Big Five companies, and I've come to understand that a lot of them either can't afford or choose not to employ numbers people. That means that accounting tasks—including the preparation of royalties statements—get assigned to people who don't understand accounting. So even if you receive your statements on time, the likelihood that they are always 100% correct is slim.

No matter how big or small your publisher is, mistakes will get made. Learn to dig into your numbers and spot mistakes.

EARNING OUT

The phrase "earning out" refers to when you will begin receiving royalties on your book. In other words, once your earnings on a book exceed the amount of the advance you were paid for that book, then your book has earned out, and you'll get royalty payments.

Some books earn out in their first or second accounting period. Some books never earn out. Some books earn out, but then unexpected high quantities of returns push the book back down into unearned territory. We'll get into some of these scenarios in a bit, but in the meantime, let's look at a rather simple example of how a book works toward earning out.

You sign a one-book contract for a $30,000 advance

and royalties of 12% of the retail price on the hardcover edition, 8% of the retail price on the trade paperback edition, and 25% of the publisher's net proceeds on the ebook edition. Your hardcover is published May 3. According to your contract, your first royalty statement will arrive in October and will reflect sales for the semiannual accounting period ending June 30.

Your first statement arrives in October as scheduled. It reflects sales for May 3 through June 30 and shows that you sold 2,000 copies of the hardcover edition and 4,000 copies of the ebook. Because your trade paperback won't release until next year, there are no sales for that edition reported on this statement.

Not bad for just under eight weeks on sale.

Before we start looking at the math and seeing how close we've come to earning out, here are a couple important things to note.

First, regarding your physical editions (the hardcover and, later, the paperback), the sales reported on your royalty statements are the number of copies your publisher shipped to distributors and retailers. They are *not* copies sold by retailers directly to readers.

Second, regarding ebook sales, 25% of *the publisher's net proceeds* (not the retail price) is the current standard royalty rate offered by the vast majority of publishers big and small. Basing ebook royalties on net proceeds rather than retail price is something that became standard over time, as a result of several factors—not the least of which is because it's harder to standardize the retail price of an ebook than it is to standardize the retail price of a hardcover or paperback. Why? Well, Amazon sells your book to Kindle readers, Barnes & Noble sells your book to Nook readers, Kobo sells your book to Kobo readers, Apple sells your book as an iBook, and so on. These ebook sellers don't buy fixed quantities of your ebook at wholesale discounts or maintain an inventory of them in a warehouse somewhere, like they do your physical editions. Rather, they serve as "agents" for ebook sales. So each accounting period, your publisher reports on your statement how much money they collected from all ebook sellers for the sale of your ebook, and they pass 25% of that figure on to you as royalties.

So getting back to our example, let's say you sold 2,000 copies of the hardcover edition, the price of which your publisher set at $24.00. That's $48,000. Yet understand that $48,000 is *not* what your publisher collected on these sales; publishers sell books to distributors and retailers at wholesale discounts of around 50% to 65%, sometimes higher. Regardless, your royalty rate is based on the retail price the publisher sets for the book, so for now, you don't have to worry about discounting—although I will touch on some pitfalls with high discounting a bit later).

According to your contract, your royalty rate on those sales is 12%. That means you've earned $5,760.

You also sold 4,000 copies of the ebook. Let's say your publisher is reporting that their net proceeds on those sales totaled $11,960. You get 25% of that, so you've earned another $2,990.

Your total earnings reported on your first statement are, therefore, $8,750 (the $5,760 you earned for sales of the hardcover edition plus the $2,990 you earned for sales of the ebook). Because your original advance was $30,000, you haven't earned out yet. Subtract $30,000 from the $8,750 you've earned so far, and you'll arrive at your unearned balance of -$21,250.

This figure should also be the *beginning balance on your next statement.* Make sure that your ending and beginning balances match from one statement to the next!

RESERVES AND RETURNS

The example above is relatively simplified. To get real, let's complicate it a bit by talking about reserves and returns.

First, understand that most distributors and retailers only buy books from publishers on a returnable basis. That means that they can return unsold copies to your publisher at any time for a refund. If they bought copies of your book on a non-returnable basis, they probably bought them at what's called high discount. Your royalties for copics sold at high discount will be calculated differently—most likely as a percentage of net proceeds rather than on retail price.

So it's still October, and you're still looking at your first royalty statement. Specifically, you're looking at the sales for your hardcover edition, and this is what you see:

- Sales: 2,000 units x $24.00 retail x 12% = $5,760
- Reserves: -900 units x $24.00 retail x 12% = -$2,592
- Total Earnings (Hardcover): $3,168

What the heck? Now, your unearned balance (once you add in your $2,990 in ebook earnings and subtract your $30,000 advance) is -$24,020 instead of only -$21,250. Why?

Reserves are your publisher's way of cushioning the blow when the inevitable returns roll in during subsequent accounting periods. Here, your publisher is letting you know that you sold 2,000 copies of the hardcover edition, but they are holding 900 of those sales "in reserves." In other words, they are withholding your earnings on those copies *for now* because their best guess is that around 900 copies will be returned to their warehouse in the coming months.

Basically, by holding reserves, your publisher is avoiding a situation in which your book earns out in its first accounting period, triggering a royalties payment to you, but then unexpectedly high returns during subsequent accounting periods push your account balance back under the line into unearned territory. If the publisher paid you royalties for that first period, you wouldn't have to return the money (just as you never have to pay the publisher back for any portion of an advance if a book doesn't earn out). But the amount they paid you for royalties for that first period would be added to your unearned balance, and your future earnings would have a greater sum to chip away at before you started getting royalties checks again. If your book never earns out again, then your publisher will have to add the amount of the royalties they paid you to whatever portion of your advance remains unearned, and write the sum off as a loss.

Note that some publishers express reserves in terms of both copies sold and those copies' related earnings, as shown in the example above. Other publishers simply express reserves as a dollar amount subtracted from total earnings on your statement's summary page. Both are fine. However your publisher chooses to express reserves on their royalty statements:

- Make sure your contract states that the publisher may not hold reserves against earnings on electronic editions of your book. Reserves are specific to the bulk return of physical editions, so publishers who want to hold reserves on digital sales are practicing creative accounting. Never a good sign.

- Watch future statements for the reserves to be released. Most Big Five will drop reserves to $0 within about two years (or four accounting periods) following a particular physical edition's initial publication date. But every book is different. Just keep an eye on it.

When I was new to royalties auditing, I noticed that one of the Big Five was holding reserves on its books far longer than four accounting periods—in fact, well after returns of those books had slowed to a trickle. After a couple conversations with this publisher's in-house accounting folks, I found out that whatever software they were using wasn't well equipped to trigger reserves adjustments. No problem. I just knew that each period I had to spend extra time on that publisher's statements, comparing reserves to actual returns and calling their accounting department to ask for adjustments...and then watching six months later when the next round of statements came to make sure those adjustments actually got made. Usually, they did.

In our example, let's look at what might happen with reserves and returns in the second accounting period.

Now it's April and you've just received your second

statement, this one for sales made between July 1 and December 31. Here's what you see in the section for your hardcover edition:

- Sales: 800 units x $24.00 retail x 12% = $2,304
- Returns: -700 units x $24.00 retail x 12% = -$2,017
- Reserves Released: 900 units x $24.00 retail x 12% = $2,592
- Reserves Held: -200 units x $24.00 retail x 12% = -$576
- Period Earnings: $2,303
- Prior Earnings: $3,168
- Cumulative Earnings: $5,471

Note that you sold 800 more copies. Yay! Why not more? Because most distributors and retailers placed their orders for your hardcover edition before it was published; that's why you saw so many sales on that first statement. But hardcovers, in general, have a relatively short life. Rarely are a hardcover's sales going to trend up from one statement to the next.

There were also some returns on this second statement (700 copies). See how your publisher released 700 copies from reserves to zero out the negative earnings associated with those returns? They expressed that release in two line items: First, they zeroed out the reserves by crediting your account with the earnings on all 900 copies they held last period. Second, they created a new line item to express that this period, they are going to hold 200 copies in reserves. That means they're still anticipating a few more returns to roll in before the end of the period.

Reserves can be difficult to understand, but when you see that they exist to soften the negative impact of returns, they can actually be kind of comforting. Some final things to note regarding reserves and returns:

- It's a best practice to track your reserves from one statement to the next and make sure your publisher is releasing them in quantities commensurate with actual returns. Don't be afraid to ask your agent to nudge your publisher to release some of your reserves.

- Over time, watch to make sure that neither reserves nor returns exceeds the total number of units sold. I've seen Big Five statements report, for example, a cumulative total of 500 copies sold but 600 returned. I've also seen Big Five statements report reserves held on editions not yet published; in other words, 0 cumulative units sold, $0 cumulative dollars earned, but reserves held on that edition of, say $1,000. How is that possible? This sort of thing is typically the result of human error and quickly resolved with a phone call. But if you're the one to find such oddities on your statements, *do not* assume you're just reading the statement wrong. Speak up!

- If your book gets off to a slow start, with moderate sales for the first year or two, it's likely your publisher will release all reserves. However, if something happens later to rapidly boost sales, like the announcement of a movie deal, then your publisher might begin to hold reserves again. Totally normal. Just start tracking reserves against actual returns again like you did before.

- In tracking and graphing sales for each book we represent, I've noticed a recurring phenomenon I call "the second-period slump." That means that regardless of how robust your sales were on your first statement, you should brace yourself for the second statement, which will inevitably contain returns. If you're a writer who only looks at the bottom line, this can be depressing, or even alarming. But if you're a writer who understands the numbers, and how publishing and bookselling work, then the second-period slump is no big deal. The good news is, you'll probably see a rebound on your third statement, and by your fourth, you'll have a fairly clear view of your book's initial success in the market.

- If your initial edition was a hardcover, and your hardcover sold relatively well in its first few months, then (depending on your genre and market) your publisher will most likely move ahead with publishing your trade paperback edition. It's typical for the trade paperback to release about one year after the hardcover (sometimes sooner), and your trade paperback will sell tons more copies and earn you tons more money. We often say that the life of a book is decided by how well the paperback sells. So probably on your third statement, you'll see three things: (a) a sharp drop-off in sales of the hardcover, (b) big returns of the hardcover, as booksellers make room on their shelves for the trade paperback, and (c) a new line item expressing trade paperback sales, complete with this edition's appropriate royalty rate and subentries for returns and reserves.

JOINT VERSUS SEPARATE ACCOUNTING

Here's a sticky issue. On contracts for two or more books, publishers will often push for what's called "joint accounting." This means that they don't have to pay you royalties for *any* books on the contract until *all* books on the contract earn out their advances.

For example, let's say you have a two-book contract for $10,000 per book ($20,000 total). Book I earns out its $10,000 advance within a year. In fact, it earned exactly

$14,328. That means you should get a royalties check for $3,678.80 ($4,328 less your agent's 15% commission), right?

Not if your agent granted the publisher joint accounting during the deal or contract negotiation! Under joint accounting, that $4,328 gets rolled over against the $10,000 advance for Book II. Now, instead of earning royalties on Book I, you're stuck with an unearned balance of -$5,672 for both books on the contract combined. And, unfortunately for you, if Book II flops and never earns out, you'll never see a dime in royalties for *either* book on the contract.

If your agent is negotiating a multi-book deal for you, make sure they're holding firm on getting you separate accounting. If your first book earns out its advance, then you should be earning royalties on it, whether subsequent books on the contract earn out or not.

ESCALATORS

Your agent might negotiate a royalties escalator for you, or perhaps, in an auction, an editor might offer a royalties escalator to sweeten their offer. An escalator simply increases your royalty rate as more copies of your book are sold.

For instance, a typical escalator for a young-adult trade paperback might be structured like this: 7.5% of the retail price on the first 10,000 copies sold and 8% on all copies sold thereafter. For a hardcover release in the adult market, a three-tier escalator might be 10% on the first 5,000 copies sold, 12.5% on the next 5,000 copies (to 10,000 total copies sold), and 15% on all copies sold thereafter.

If your contract includes a royalties escalator for a particular edition, make sure you are keeping track of the total copies sold of that edition from one period to the next. Once the cumulative number climbs up over the threshold for the escalator, make sure the escalator kicks in and that you have begun earning the higher rate. However, note that some publishers don't count the copies of that edition they sold to wholesalers at high discount—only copies sold through regular distribution channels count toward triggering an escalator.

SUBRIGHTS ROYALTIES

A lot of newer authors grossly underestimate the revenue available to them through subrights sales. Whether your *publisher* is making those sales on your behalf or your *agent* is, subrights earnings mean additional statements and more opportunities for accounting errors to get made.

First, let's look at what happens when your *publisher* sells your subrights.

Let's say that in your original contract, you granted your publisher world rights (meaning they can sell translation rights to foreign publishers) as well as audio rights. Your publisher's subrights department sells your book to publishers in three foreign territories—France, Germany, and Taiwan—and to Audible here in the US, who will produce the English-language audiobook. That's four subrights deals.

The contracts for these deals are between your publisher (not you!) and each of the four entities who are buying the rights from your publisher to produce their own editions of your book. Neither you nor your agent will have a hand in these negotiations. So how do your earnings on these editions make it back to you?

On your next royalty statement from your publisher, you'll see four new line items: one for France, one for Germany, one for Taiwan, and one for Audible. (Usually, subrights earnings are itemized on the last page of a royalty statement.) Some publishers express copies sold by those publishers as well as monies earned, but many only express monies earned.

Your next step is to page through your original contract and find the list of all the subrights splits you agreed to—the percentages you and your publisher will earn on various types of subrights deals. Depending on how your agent negotiated your contract, you can expect that your share of earnings on subrights deals will fall between 50% and 80%.

Let's say that according to your contract, you're due a 50% share of audio earnings and a 75% share of foreign-rights earnings. That means as soon as your publisher receives the advance they negotiated from Audible—let's say it was $7,500—you'll see 50% of that ($3,750) on your next royalty statement from your publisher. Likewise, as soon as your publisher receives the advances they negotiated from your publishers in France, Germany, and Taiwan, you'll see 75% of those amounts, reported in US dollars, on your next royalty statement from your publisher.

All your subrights earnings will be added to your statement's bottom line. Either those earnings will help chip away at your unearned balance or, if your book has earned out, they'll be rolled into the amount your publisher owes you in royalties for that period.

Now let's look the second scenario—what happens when your *agent* sells your subrights.

If your agent retained audio and translation rights, then it's up to your agent to broker these subrights deals on your behalf. So let's say your agent sells your book to Audible for that same $7,500 advance. But now, this deal was done *independent of your publisher*, so instead of the 50% split you'd earn toward your bottom line if your publisher brokered the deal, you'll get a check from your agent for $6,375—the total amount of your Audible advance less your agent's 15% commission. And you'll get this check whether or not you've earned out your advance from your US publisher.

Further, let's say your agent sells your book to those same publishers in France, Germany, and Taiwan. Again, you'll receive checks from your agent for those advances whether or not you've earned out your advance from your US publisher. Note, however, that the commissions structure for foreign deals might be different depending on whether or not your agent partnered with foreign co-agents on your behalf.

Under this second scenario, you're no longer receiving one tidy royalty statement from your US publisher twice per year, with all your earnings neatly rolled into one bottom line. Now you're receiving ten royalty statements per year. Ten! Each year, you'll get two statements from your US publisher, four statements from Audible (because they report quarterly), two statements from Germany, and one statement each from France and Taiwan (most foreign publishers process royalties only once per year, but some, like the UK, Australia/New Zealand, Germany, and Brazil, report semiannually). So while this scenario means more money for you, it also more statements for you to track down, more numbers for you to dig into—and potentially more errors for you to catch.

In summary, if your *publisher* sells your subrights, your money funnels from all your various subrights publishers to your US publisher. Then it travels from your US publisher to your agent. Then from your agent to you.

If your *agent* sells your subrights, your money funnels from your US publisher and all your various subrights publishers directly to your agent. Then from your agent to you.

INFORMATION YOU SHOULD EXPECT TO FIND ON A ROYALTY STATEMENT

Here's a list of what you should expect to see on a solid, well-prepared royalty statement:

- An opening balance, or "balance forward," expressing the same number reported as the bottom line of the previous period's statement. If your book hasn't earned out yet, the opening balance will be a negative number expressing how much more you have to earn before you begin earning royalties. If the opening balance is $0, then the book has earned out and you've already received royalties. In other words, after a book earns out, your publisher zeroes out your account every period by paying you what you're owed.

- For each edition, units sold for the current accounting period, plus cumulative or life-to-date units sold.
- For each edition, earnings for the current period, plus cumulative or life-to-date earnings.
- For each edition, the royalty rate that was applied to this period's sales. If the rate is based on retail, you'll see the publisher's set retail price. If the rate is based on net proceeds, you'll see both the total net proceeds the publisher is reporting and the percentage of those net proceeds they owe you according to your contract.
- For each edition, units returned for the current period, plus negative earnings related to those returns and the royalty rate used to figure those negative earnings.
- For each edition, reserves held/released for the current period. You may not see a line item for cumulative reserves on a given statement, but reserves should be reported in such a way that you can easily track them down to zero over a series of consecutive statements.
- Total units sold across all editions for this period, as well as cumulatively.

- Total earnings across all editions for this period, as well as cumulatively.

- A summary section containing an itemized list of all prior payments made to you by the publisher for this book. This should include all advance payments, any bonuses, and a cumulative total of all previously remitted royalties payments. Note that you may not have received your total advance by the time you receive your first royalty statement. For instance, if you're owed a portion of your advance on publication of your trade paperback edition, which won't publish until a year after your hardcover, then you will (a) receive a check for that portion when your trade paperback is published, and (b) see the amount of that check added to the "prior payments" section on your next statement.

- A bottom line expressing total cumulative earnings minus total cumulative prior payments. If the difference is negative, the book has not yet earned out, and you will receive no royalties this period. If the difference is positive, this will be the amount of royalties due. Your publisher will send your agent a check or electronic funds transfer in that amount. Your agent will pass through this amount, less their 15% commission, to you.

COMMON MISTAKES ON ROYALTY STATEMENTS

Over the years, I've seen a lot of mistakes get made on a lot of royalty statements by a lot of publishers big, medium, and small. I've helped recover somewhere in the neighborhood of $100,000 owed to our clients as a result of those mistakes. I've also seen mistakes get made in the other direction, in the author's favor. And, yes, I call those mistakes to publishers' attention as well. The goal here is always clean, transparent accounts.

To that end, here's a rundown of the most common royalties errors I come across:

- Incorrect advance amount reported.
- Incorrect royalty rates applied.
- Incorrect subrights splits applied.
- Missing advances for subrights deals. Note that it can take a year or so for an advance from a foreign publisher to show up on your royalty statement. Every time your publisher's subrights department tells you they've closed a new deal for you, add the details of that deal to your personal notes so that you can watch for the payment to appear on your statement.
- Failure of a royalty escalator to kick in. Or escalators properly applied on one statement, but dropped back down to the pre-escalator rate on the subsequent statement.

- The correct royalty rate applied to sales, but a higher rate applied to returns.
- Cumulative returns that exceed cumulative sales.
- Reserves held on editions that have not yet published, or reserves held on electronic editions.
- The opening balance on one statement not matching the ending balance on the prior statement.
- The cumulative sum of prior payments reported not matching the actual cumulative sum of payments received.
- Reserves interfering with the triggering of a bonus payment. For instance, if an author's contract includes a bonus clause that says they'll get $5,000 if they sell 10,000 copies of the hardcover edition in the twelve months following initial publication, what if the statement reports 11,000 cumulative copies sold and 200 copies held reserves, making the bottom line 9,000 copies? Remember that copies held in reserves were actually sales—you're just not getting credited for those sales quite yet. So you are officially owed that $5,000 bonus. During the negotiation of a bonus clause, your agent can request "for the avoidance of doubt" language that protects you from this situation.
- Copies sold at high discount exceeding the

limit set forth in the contract. Good agents will negotiate contract terms that limit the number of copies of your book your publisher can sell at high discount. This is in your best interest because the royalties you receive on copies sold at high discount are considerably lower than they are on copies sold through regular distribution channels. So know if your contract places limits on high-discount sales, and then watch your statements to make sure the publisher is honoring those limits. In one particular case, for one of our bestselling authors whose books have sold millions of copies and been translated into more than thirty languages, we discovered that the publisher (a Big Five) was selling tens of thousands of copies at high discount, essentially blowing the ceiling off the limit in the contract. When we called this to the publisher's attention, they immediately corrected the mistake by paying the author their regular royalty rate for every copy sold at high discount above their contracted limit. This meant that the author received a check for nearly $10,000 that they would not have received if we had not audited their royalty statement.

- Missing or misplaced editions. For instance, on a recent statement from an audio publisher, we saw sales for the physical edition (CDs), but no sales for the audio-download edition, which typically comprise the grand majority of total audiobook sales. Turns out the digital sales for that book had been incorrectly applied to a different book.

- Boxed sets being incorrectly accounted. If your publisher decides to package your trilogy in a boxed set, how will the sales be reported? Here's how one Big Five does it: If 100 boxed sets of your trilogy's trade paperback edition are sold in a given period, then you'll see 100 copies sold on your statement for Book I, 100 copies sold on your statement for Book II, and 100 copies sold on your statement for Book III. However, boxed sets are typically sold at a special price. So on your statement for Book I, in the section for the trade-paperback edition, you'll see a line item for regular sales with, say, 7.5% royalties based on a retail price of $15. But you'll also see a new line item for 100 copies sold, with 7.5% royalties based on a retail price of only $8. You see an identical line item on the statements for Book II and Book III. That's because your publisher is selling the boxed set for $24, or $8 per book instead of $15 per book. All good. What I've seen a smaller publisher do—which isn't OK—is dump all the sales of a boxed trilogy onto the statement for Book III. Why isn't that OK? Well, what if your agent got you a separate accounting clause in your contract, but the publisher is applying all the sales of your boxed set to the advance for Book III, and Book III isn't looking likely to earn out? That's basically back-door joint accounting, because you'll never see any royalties from the sale of your boxed set, which contains titles for which you should be earning royalties. Now, if the publisher, for their own ease, wants to put all the sales for the boxed set on the statement for Book I, and Book I *has* earned out, that's good news for you. Still, as I mentioned before, I much prefer clean, transparent, *correct* accounting for each book. At the end of the day, it's important to know how your publisher is handling the numbers for these sorts of things.

Again, whenever you see something weird on a royalty statement, ask. Your agent, or someone who works for your agent, should be able to either explain what you're looking at or confirm that a mistake has been made, and then take steps to get it corrected in a timely manner.

STEP 16

OUT OF PRINT AND REVERSION OF RIGHTS

A PUBLISHING CONTRACT SHOULD NEVER BE IN EFFECT for life. All publishing contracts should expire at some point, with all rights granted therein reverting to the grantor—you. Let's look at the various ways that can happen.

First, your contract should contain an out-of-print clause. *If it doesn't, do not sign it.* The purpose of the out-of-print clause is to lay out all the conditions that must be met before your book will be considered out-of-print, at which point you can get your rights back.

The out-of-print conditions should be both clear and attainable. *Never sign a contract if you do not understand the conditions or if you suspect that they are unattainable.*

Unfortunately, there are some sneaky publishers out there; they'll take advantage of the fact that not all authors—nor all agents!—know how to recognize when the out-of-print conditions spelled out in the contract are things that are never going to happen. Like sales falling below a particular threshold.

So let's talk about thresholds.

THRESHOLDS AND TERMS OF LICENSE

The life of most contracts done in the US, Canada, the UK, and Australia/New Zealand is based on sales thresholds. These contracts require that your book's sales fall below a certain threshold (usually 250-350 copies in any two consecutive six-month accounting periods) before you can request a reversion of rights. Your request might be denied, depending on what other out-of-print conditions are laid out in your contract, but you can ask.

Your agent should negotiate to get your out-of-print threshold on the high end of that range. Why? Well, a publisher doesn't have to try very hard to sell 250 copies of your book in a year, so there's no incentive for them to promote your book. They can just let it languish, and the copies that sell here and there over the course of a year will probably exceed 250, if barely. Some publishers open contract negotiations with a 100-copy threshold. Absurd.

If, however, a publisher has to sell 350 copies of your book every year to keep your book in print, then they have to work a little harder, or they have to revert the rights to you.

Thresholds are most often based on cumulative units sold across all editions *produced by the publisher*, which excludes editions published by third-party entities, i.e., editions published as a result of subrights deals. In other words, your publisher can't include sales of your large-print edition or German audiobook when they're adding up total unit sales to determine how far above or below the out-of-print threshold your book is. Sometimes, however, thresholds are based on earnings, as in once the author's cumulative earnings fall below, say, $500 in any two consecutive six-month accounting periods, the book may be deemed out of print and the author may request a reversion.

The life of most foreign contracts, on the other hand, is based not on thresholds but on term-of-license. These contracts will state that, say, five or six or however many years from the date of the contract, the agreement simply ends and all rights automatically revert to the author. Easy peasy. Some smaller presses or specialty publishers here in the US operate that way, too, and there's nothing wrong with that.

REQUESTING A REVERSION OF RIGHTS

When you notice that your book's sales have fallen below threshold, go ahead and ask your agent to request a reversion of rights. Most contracts specify that this request must be made in writing (we typically send our requests via certified mail so that we have proof the publisher received them). Most contracts also specify that once the publisher receives this request, they will have a period of time—usually three months—to decide how to respond. That's because most Big Five hold their reversion-review meetings once per quarter.

Maybe your publisher will respond with, "Oh, yeah! This book did pretty well back when we were actively promoting it, and the author has a new series coming out next year, which will undoubtedly lead readers to discover *this* book. Let's hold onto rights for now, order another print run, and put some marketing muscle behind it."

Or maybe they'll simply agree to revert the rights and send you an official reversion letter. If that's the case, then all the rights you granted to your publisher in your original contract will once again belong to you. You'll be free to do whatever you want with your book, including self-publishing it or selling the rights to a small press who publishes reprints.

If your publisher sold subrights to your book, then even if they agree in writing to terminate their contract with you, the contracts they signed with third-party publishers on your behalf will remain in effect until *those* contracts' terms of license expire. Your official reversion letter from your publisher will probably spell out which subrights agreements are still in effect and for how long; if not, simply have your agent call your publisher and get those dates of expiry for you. Always make it your business to know who holds your rights and for how long.

REMAINDERING

When a particular physical edition of your book is no longer selling well, then your publisher will decide to remainder it. They'll either destroy the extra copies or sell them at deep discount to a clearinghouse. Basically, they're cleaning out their warehouse.

But not before they give you the chance to buy some or all of those copies at cost.

Your publisher will send your agent a remainder notice, and your agent will then forward it to you. This notice lists exactly which edition is being remaindered and when—maybe 30 or 60 days from now. The notice will also contain an order form that you can fill out and send back to your publisher, if you want to. You don't have to, but if you're an author who makes a lot of appearances and does a lot of handselling, then buying extra copies at cost might be a good idea. You might even place these copies for sale on consignment at local independent bookstores.

When we receive a remainder notice at the agency, we immediately look at the last two royalty statements for that book to see how close sales are to threshold. If sales are under threshold, we ask the author if they would like us to request reversion. If it's a yes, then we'll prepare the official reversion-request letter, citing both the threshold and the remainder notice as reasons the publisher should revert rights.

Oftentimes, however, a publisher's decision to remainder a particular edition has little to do with how well a title is currently selling. For instance, a publisher might remainder your hardcover edition while your trade paperback is still going gangbusters, simply because no one's buying your hardcover anymore and it's just gathering dust in the warehouse. Nevertheless, remaindering is something that should nudge you to assess where your book is on its path to reversion.

OTHER OUT-OF-PRINT CONDITIONS

Terms of license are fairly cut and dry—a certain date comes, and the contract is automatically terminated, with all rights automatically reverting to the author.

Thresholds are a little trickier because they rarely stand alone. In other words, thresholds are often only one of *several* conditions that must *all* be met before the publisher is bound to revert your rights. Again, all this should be spelled out in your contract's out-of-print clause, so be sure to read it carefully.

One condition you might see is something like this: *The book shall be deemed in print if it is listed as available for sale in the publisher's catalog.* That used to make sense back when publishers printed their catalogs twice a year and physically handed them to book buyers and subrights brokers. But what about now, when publishers' catalogs are posted on their websites? Why would they ever remove a book from that unlimited digital space? If all a publisher has to do to deem your book "in print" is list it on their website, are you ever going to get your rights back? Only if the publisher is feeling generous.

Another condition you might come across: *The book shall be deemed in print if copies of any physical edition are available for purchase in the publisher's inventory.* That means that even if your sales have fallen below threshold, if your publisher still has a couple dusty boxes of your paperback edition stashed away in some dark, forgotten corner of their warehouse, they don't have to grant you a reversion of rights. Some will. But they don't have to.

In these cases, if you send the publisher a reversion request, they might offer to sell you, the author, the remaining stock at cost. This would bring their inventory down to zero, satisfying *this particular* out-of-print condition. But even if you believe you have also satisfied all the other out-of-print conditions in your contract, the publisher will never come out and say, "If you buy the remaining stock, then we will revert your rights." Instead, they'll say, "If you buy the remaining stock, then you can feel free to submit another reversion request, and our rights team will review it when they meet again to discuss reversions next quarter."

This is a typical situation and a common practice. Some authors roll the dice and pony up the cost for the books. Others sigh and resign themselves to the fact that they'll probably never get their rights back.

To my thinking, this practice is absolutely egregious.

Agents should negotiate contract terms that prevent publishers from even mentioning their inventory levels in their definitions of in-print or out-of-print. After all, the author gets zero say in how many copies of the physical editions a publisher orders from the printer. What if they order an initial print run of 10,000 copies, but five years later only 2,000 ever sold? Is it reasonable for the publisher to hold onto those non-lucrative rights until the author buys up 8,000 copies of their own book? I think not.

The good news is, most publishers are reasonable and evaluate their reversion requests on a book-by-book basis. They may decide to revert rights to a book (and often do) even if not all the out-of-print conditions spelled out in the contract for that book have been met. The point is, they are not legally bound to. Some publishers will cling tooth and nail to every right they've been granted, whether they're making any money on those rights or not. That's why it's important to ensure that the conditions written into your out-of-print clause are attainable—not just one or two of those conditions, but all of them together. And *that's* why it pays to have an agent who understands how to negotiate reasonable out-of-print conditions for you.

A FINAL WORD

YOUR CAREER, YOUR FUTURE

EVERY WRITER'S PATH IS DIFFERENT. SOME HIT IT BIG with their debut novel and enjoy long-term success. Or they never write again. Or they write plenty but never publish again. Some hit the *New York Times* bestseller list and then stall. Others get a huge advance and are anointed as the Next Big Thing, only to fizzle out. Some claw their way up the ladder and make it to the top. Others spend years working toward their goals of landing an agent or a Big Five deal, and then they give up. Or they don't. Or they find success in ways they didn't even know existed when they started their journeys: through independent publishing, through small, mid-sized, or academic presses, through collaboration, through switching forms or genres.

Every path is different because every writer defines success in their own way: how many books they sell, how much money they make, whether their earnings will allow them to quit their day job, how many reviews they get, what events they're invited to speak at, what awards they win or bestseller lists they land on.

Whatever your goal, however you define success, remember that it all starts—*and constantly circles back to*—the writing. How much do you write? How willing are you to continue improving your craft? How committed are you to the writing process? How focused can you stay on doing your best work day in and day out when those unexpected trees crash down across your path?

Whether after reading this book you choose to pursue the representation of a literary agent who can guide you through the world of traditional-publishing or not, I sincerely hope you now feel better equipped to make the best decision for you. For your books and readers. For your career.

Go forth, write good books, and publish!

APPENDIX

RECOMMENDED RESOURCES

James Scott Bell • *Plot and Structure: Techniques and Exercises for Crafting a Plot that Grips Readers from Start to Finish*

James Scott Bell • *Revision and Self-Editing: Techniques for Transforming Your First Draft into a Finished Novel*

James Scott Bell • *Write Your Novel from the Middle: A New Approach for Plotters, Pantsers, and Everyone in Between*

Jessica Brody • *Save the Cat! Writes a Novel: The Last Book on Novel Writing You'll Ever Need*

Larry Brooks • *Story Engineering: Mastering the 6 Core Competencies of Successful Writing*

Lisa Cron • *Story Genius: How to Use Brain Science to Go Beyond Outlining and Write a Riveting Novel (Before*

You Waste Three Years Writing 327 Pages That Go Nowhere)

Lisa Cron • *Wired for Story: The Writer's Guide to Using Brain Science to Hook Readers from the Very First Sentence*

David Farland • *Million Dollar Outlines*

John Gardner • *The Art of Fiction: Notes on Craft for Young Writers*

Ursula K. Le Guin • *Steering the Craft: A Twenty-First Century Guide to Sailing the Sea of Story*

Francine Prose • *Reading Like a Writer: A Guide for People Who Love Books and for Those Who Want to Write Them*

John Truby • *The Anatomy of Story: 22 Steps to Becoming a Master Storyteller*

Christopher Vogler • *The Writer's Journey: Mythical Structure for Writers*

ABOUT THE AUTHOR

Angie Hodapp is the Director of Literary Development at Nelson Literary Agency. A graduate of the Publishing Institute at the University of Denver, she holds a BA in English education and an MA in English with an emphasis in communication development. She has worked in language education and professional writing and editing for more than twenty years and is a frequent presenter at writing conferences and literary events. Dedicated to helping writers improve their craft and learn about the ever-changing publishing industry, Angie is the author of the Writer-in-the-Know series.

www.ingramcontent.com/pod-product-compliance
Lightning Source LLC
Chambersburg PA
CBHW060458280326
41933CB00014B/2788